Co-Creators with God

Co-Creators with God

Creative Strategies for Faith Formation

BERNADETTE T. STANKARD

Twenty-Third Publications
A Division of Bayard
One Montauk Avenue, Suite 200
New London, CT 06320
(860) 437-3012 or (800) 321-0411
www.23rdpublications.com

ISBN 978-1-58595-584-8
Library of Congress Catalog Card Number: 2006920448
Printed in the U.S.A.

Contents

Introduction

For well over thirty years I have worked with catechists and parents, teachers and children. It has been an exciting, uplifting time for me, except when I listen to that familiar line: "I can't do what you do. I'm not creative."

Creativity is a gift from God we all have. Sadly, many of us don't believe we have this wonderful gift. Instead we choose to believe others are more talented, more creative, more expressive than we are. The reality is *we* are creative. God made us in the image and likeness of God. Since God is Creator, it follows that we share in the creative action of God. We will use this gift of creativity if we are willing to let the image of God shine through us.

Unfortunately many of us were taught in a school system that squelched creativity. We learned to memorize. We learned to read. We learned to add, subtract, multiply, and divide. But perhaps we didn't learn to trust our own interests and thoughts and our God-given talents and curiosity. We forgot how to play while learning. We put away our explorer hats and forgot how to be comfortable while being foolish in trying new things. Even in our life of faith we may have let creativity slip away. The temptation is to fall into tried and true ways of approaching God and lose the sense of wonder that brings us closer to the Creator.

This book is an attempt to reawaken and strengthen creativity in each of you, especially with regard to your faith. It will help you look at God and the people of your faith community in a new and different way. You will look at the things that prevent you from being creative, as well as what you need to consider if you want to grow in creativity. Most of all you will discover ways to trust your own creative gifts once again, and draw closer to God, the ultimate Creator.

My suggestion is that you put aside judgment as you read this book. Reflect carefully on the ideas. Consider all the questions. Try some of the exercises. Finally, when you put the book down, think about what you have read. Keep what you find helpful, and set aside whatever you feel doesn't apply to you right now. Feel free to reread those sections at a future time, and see if your reaction to them has changed. By following this procedure you can open yourself to the creative power of our Creator. You will see for yourself the gentle but powerful changes that will begin to occur in your faith life.

A newborn infant babbles, gurgles, wriggles, and reaches out to touch the world. Hopefully this book will serve as a catalyst for all of us to experience the wonder of that first day of life again and again, each time we are creative.

> God said, "Let there be light"; and there was light. And God saw that the light was good; and God separated the light from the darkness. God called the light Day, and the darkness he called Night. And there was evening and there was morning, the first day.
>
> Genesis 1:3–5

CHAPTER 1

Discoveries of Creation

And on the seventh day God finished the work that he had done, and he rested on the seventh day from all the work that he had done. So God blessed the seventh day and hallowed it, because on it God rested from all the work that he had done in creation.

Genesis 2:2–3

And on the eighth day, God continued his work of creation with man and woman. First God pondered over the food he had given them to eat. He admired the funny avocado and the juicy tomato, squeezed the orange and let the sweet juice run down his chin while he relished the taste. God watched as Eve pulled carrots out of the ground and washed them in the stream. God laughed as Adam tried his hand at a pomegranate, experimenting with what part to eat and what not.

While God was laughing, he slipped and fell to the ground, crushing a number of cherries that had fallen to the earth. The sweet substance inside was spilled from their tiny casings. And then God had an idea. Why not crush some fruit and mix it together, something that would be a cross between the whole fruit and the juice that God could still taste on his chin? And then God called Eve over and began to tell her his idea. Eve nodded, recognizing all the possibilities in this crushed fruit. Together God and Eve crushed cherry upon cherry, mixing the fruit together, removing the pits, and finally enjoying a moment of taste testing.

God scrunched up his mouth. "Bitter! No one will want to have that spread on their meat or the bread we will learn to make." Eve nodded in agreement. At that moment Adam raced over, excited over his new discovery.

"Look, God! Look, Eve! Look at this silly stick. I broke one by mistake and this gooey stuff came out and I tasted it. It is so sweet! Surely this was meant to be used with something," he said, peeling back more of the bark.

And then God looked at Eve, Eve looked at God, and both smiled.

"We know just the thing it should be mixed with," said God. So God and Eve and Adam began to peel back the bark and crush the sweet sugar cane, mixing it carefully with the cherries.

"Ah, just right," said God, smacking his lips. He looked over at Adam and Eve. "Of course, there will be better jellies made by grandmas and aunts hundreds of years hence, but this, this," he said holding up the bowl of cherry jelly, "this is the creation that will make all that possible."

The Hues of Creation

God laughed and moved away to inspect more of last week's creation. God moved through the fields full of color and played with names for the different hues spread out in profusion. Fuchsia sounded like a fun word, as did magenta and ultramarine. Name after name rolled off God's tongue. Overhead, birds and other flying creatures punctuated the blue—or was it turquoise or cobalt or indigo? In the distance God could see the cows—what an interesting name Adam had chosen for these creatures that now slowly chewed the grass. Earlier they had allowed Adam to pull at their udders to bring milk into the world for the first time.

God climbed a hill, relishing the different rocks and bugs and flowers. At the summit God took a deep breath and gazed at the surroundings, thinking mightily. Horses romped in the distance. One paused to race another and God thought, "Ah, racing them at some future time. Good sport." God saw the lightning flash of a distant storm start a fire and thought, "Our jelly might be better heated and then cooled." Looking out on all the good things of the past week of creation, God was filled with more and more ideas. How would people share these ideas from one generation to another? Why, God thought, they would invent the alphabet. Surely his people would have enough creative ideas to fill many books. God chuckled. Fill many books? Yes, maybe even a whole series of books, which years later would be called encyclopedias.

Ice Cream and Cotton

Suddenly a breathless Eve ran up the hill.

"God! God! Come quickly. It's Adam! Something is the matter with Adam."

Without hesitation, God scooped up Eve and leaped down the hill in the direction she had pointed. Sure enough, God saw Adam shaking even more than trees caressed by the strongest wind.

"Whatever is the matter, Adam?" God looked at Adam. The little goosebumps on his flesh caused God to smile knowingly. "You went over toward the penguins where the coldest air is, right?"

Adam nodded, his chattering teeth adding emphasis.

"Whatever for?" God asked.

Adam managed to say that in the morning when he had milked the cows, he had an idea. Perhaps if he took the milk to a cold place, he and Eve might have something solid to eat that tasted like milk but wasn't milk.

God said, "You were trying to make ice cream, weren't you?"

Adam looked puzzled.

"Never mind," God said, thinking that eventually the human race would have thirty-two flavors and more of this iced milk delight.

God pulled Adam closer to him. "Now, for something to warm you up while I'm busy with something else." God puzzled for a few seconds, then his glance fell on a vast field of cotton plants. "Hmmm." He tapped Eve on the shoulder. "Would you gather a bunch of that cotton and bring it here?"

Eve was off in a flash. Before God could even say, "It was very good," she was back with a bundle of the fluffy white balls. Next God instructed Eve to put together several sticks to form a grid. While Eve worked, God firmly held Adam and with the other hand pulled and stretched the cotton into long strings.

"Here, Eve," God said, "weave these back and forth through the grid." Eve did so and, in the blink of God's eye, a long flowing white piece of cloth lay at their feet. God reach over and covered Adam with it.

"It's a shame to cover such a beautiful piece of handiwork like your body, Adam," God said. "But when you venture into the cold, you are going to need something to cover your body so you don't freeze. This cotton blanket will keep you very warm indeed." God turned to Eve, whose eyes were dancing with ideas. "Yes, Eve, sometime in the future there will be dresses and pants and shoes and all sorts of adornments to keep your body warm. In the meantime can we try some of that ice cream?"

So God and Adam and Eve walked off toward the penguins and, with plates of ice cream, talked about all the possibilities of jelly and horses, of birds and colors, of ice cream and clothes.

That night they all lay down together, with the stars twinkling overhead, the cry of the loon in the distance, and the gentle lap of water caressing the sandy bank. They spoke of their day and of the days to come.

"You know," God said, just as they were about to drift off, "perhaps tomorrow we can try to make the cotton different colors, from white to blue or yellow or...."

"The red onion," Eve interrupted, "would make such a beautiful red color."

"Good night," said Adam, as he pulled his white cotton blanket tighter around him.

God and Adam and Eve saw that all they had made was very good. And there was evening and morning, the eighth day.

CHAPTER 2

Life, the Creative Moment

My mother was born in Poland at the turn of the twentieth century, in a small town outside of Warsaw. She wasn't born in a hospital or at home; rather, she was born in a field during harvest time. Her mother, busy gathering the fruits of the summer, had been having labor pains throughout the day. Finally, when she knew it was time, she moved away from the other women. Alone, in the middle of a field with only butterflies and sunshine bearing witness, she gave birth to her second child, my mother.

In order to look at creation and our ability to share in God's creativity, we have to look at life as the sum total of creativity. We will look at the time of birth as the beginning of our journey toward the wholeness of creation. This moment of creation is universally shared by women and men across cultures. New life is confirmation once again of the power of God. In this miracle of life, our creativity rises with beauty and wonder.

The Beginning of Our Share in Creation

Every woman's experience of birth labor is different. Consequently each approach is as creative and unique as the person giving birth. In many countries women squat to give birth. Others, like the Tapirape women of Brazil, lie in string hammocks, legs hung over the sides with a slit cut in the hammock to accommodate the new child's entry into the world. In Mexico, the Mixtecan Indian women kneel with their knees wide apart on a specially made straw mat, while their partners hold them around the waist.

Midwives and husbands devise individual ways to make the birthing process more comfortable for the mother. In Bang Chan, Thailand, a husband offers his body as a leaning post and while his wife leans against him for support, he digs his toes into her thighs, giving her some relief from the pressures elsewhere in her body. In rural areas of the Sudan, midwives hang a rope from the ceiling of the birthing room and the mother pulls down on it during contractions. In the American Southwest, Zuni women would give birth lying on their sides facing the midwife. During contractions, the mother would pull on the midwife's belt while another person would put pressure on the woman's lower back, easing the pain.

Think of that moment of birth. The pain. The elation. The unique creation. A tiny wisp of hair is seen at the opening of the vagina. It appears. It disappears. It reappears. The mother feels a powerful urge to push, to bring this child into the world. The burning sensation heightens and the woman tries to relax, allowing the skin around the birth opening to stretch. Gradually the skin stretches under the pressure of the child's head, and finally comes the moment of birth. The head emerges, then the shoulders slide out. The father is in awe of this creation in which he has taken part. A new life, a re-enactment of that first creation. We are there, walking alongside God, sharing creation with the Eternal Wonder.

Creation is life. From that first moment of creation in Genesis, God empowered the world with the ability to create. From that moment on we would live with God and bring different creations into the world, always with the strong hand of God gifting and guiding us to completion. Whether it be the birth of a child, with the numerous and various ways of approaching that moment of beauty, or the process by which individuals learn math or science or the ABCs, we share with God in the act of creation, in realizing an idea, an invention, or a thought that breathes new life into the world.

The Kaleidoscope of Life

The famous American comedians, Bud Abbott and Lou Costello, had a comedy skit popular in the 1940s, that spoke of the importance of creating and of looking at things in a new light. In the sketch Costello meets his landlord in the hall outside his apartment. The landlord tells him that the amount of rent Costello had paid, $21, was not equal to the amount of rent owed, thirteen weeks at seven dollars a week. Costello argues with him, pointing out that he gave the landlord twenty-one dollars, which was the amount of the rent. The landlord disagrees, and the fun begins. First Lou divides the figures. Through some slick maneuvering he comes up with twenty-one. Still not convinced, the landlord wants him to do multiplication. Lou does, seven times thirteen, putting seven times one in the first column instead of the second. Naturally it adds up to twenty-one. Finally the landlord insists on addition. Lou obliges by putting seven thirteens in a column. Quickly he adds the threes and then adds each of the ones coming up with—what else? Twenty-one. A truly creative comedy sketch.

Lou Costello opened the eyes of many people to new ways of looking at things, of creating unusual approaches to solving problems, of looking beyond the black and white and seeing the gray. Dorothy Gilman, in her book *The Clairvoyant Countess*, talks about the kaleidoscope of life. Madame Karitska, her main character, says we all look through the same kaleidoscope, but it is up to us or life circumstances to turn the kaleidoscope so that we can look at the same situation, the same event, the same day with a new view.

The act of creation involves moving that kaleidoscope. We are all called to turn the kaleidoscope so that we follow our true calling as co-creators with God.

Life is *the* creative moment. Julia Cameron writes in her book, *The Artist's Way*: "Creativity is the natural order of life. Life is energy, pure creative energy." God made it that way from that first moment when God said, "Let there be light." God is the creative power infusing all of life, including us. We often forget we are a creation of God. We received our breath of life, our breath of creativity as a gift from God. It only follows that we should then continue creating, by calling forth that gift we have been given by God to be creative.

Lots of times we use that gift without knowing or reflecting on the fact that we are doing it. We do it when we rise or eat or sleep. We have the opportunity daily to be creative. Do you follow the same order each morning in putting your clothes on? Do you follow the same ritual after your shower each day? Do you eat the same breakfast? Even a small variable in these routines is a witness to new life because when you are aware of what you are doing, you are in an act of creation.

In the larger issues of life, we are creative in different ways. Each time we are faced with the search for a new occupation, each time we welcome a new life, each time we say goodbye to one another, we create. Recently a good friend's husband lost his job. After the initial turmoil of the loss, he and his wife began to approach the situation with creativity. The husband began to look at his interests and to determine whether employment similar to the one he lost was really what he wanted. After considering the possibilities, he began to apply for a wide variety of situations, always thinking that "this would be something interesting to do." His wife looked for ways to cut spending during this time of upheaval. She found that she enjoyed the challenge of being thrifty, which the change in their lives necessitated. When no job materialized quickly for her husband, she began to look for work for herself. She was surprised to find a job that offered her a chance to exercise her own creativity by working with mentally challenged adults. What began as a great loss for their family materialized into a creative adventure for the couple. Both were responding to the call to share in creation with God.

These acts of creation, of life, are repeated in thousands of varied scenarios. The young mother who needs to entertain a group of preschoolers finds that empty cardboard tubes and glitter can turn the ordinary into magical, extraordinary wands. The businessman who desires to pursue a career in writing finds that he can meet with his writing buddy once every week at lunch and so remain motivated and inspired. The woman whose mother is coping with Alzheimer's finds new ways to help stimulate her mom's mind. The man who loses his wife to cancer plans a funeral that celebrates her life, complete with clowns and her favorite music. All of these are ways of using our creativity, becoming aware of creativity as life itself.

The "Ah Ha" Moment

In addition to these times of inspiration in both the ordinary and extraordinary events of life, we are all aware of those special moments when the pieces of life seem to fall together, if only for a short time. Or we recall those times when insight strikes suddenly and we experience a kind of revelation—the "ah ha" moments.

A writer friend talked of an "ah ha" moment she experienced at 3 AM one morning. She had been struggling over what to do about her job. As a teacher, she had had a difficult year in a school where the children ranged from the very rich to the very poor. The parents were always on the side of their kids, who could do no wrong. She tried to decide whether or not to leave. Was she abandoning the kids who needed her? Was she giving in to the parents' demands? Perhaps she would be leaving the children without at least one adult who would hold them accountable. She also realized that the job was causing a great deal of tension in her own family life. She yelled at her children and her husband over small matters. She had no time for them since so much was given over to school work. She was a mother and wife in name only.

As she twisted and turned in bed that morning, unable to fall asleep again, she looked over at her husband with whom she had fought just before going to sleep. He hadn't done anything except forget to get milk, an oversight easily remedied by a late-night run to the grocery store. This is ridiculous, she thought. I never used to be this way. Pictures of her own children played through her mind. Her daughters were becoming more nervous and seemed to walk on eggshells around her. Her two sons were getting into more trouble than she ever thought they would. And what about herself? I'm miserable, she thought. I don't feel like God's around. I don't like the way I am treating my kids or my husband. And then the realization hit her. I'm taking care of everyone else's family but my own. She realized that she was allowing her concern for the children at the school to overshadow her care of her own family. She knew another teacher would come, a teacher that nine times out of ten would be a good teacher for the group, one who would care as much, if not more, than she did. Other persons could teach at the school, but she couldn't give her family responsibilities over to another woman. She was called to fulfill them. This was her family. God had called her to this role on her wedding day fifteen years ago.

She felt peace sweep over her. She knew what she needed to do. She leaned over and kissed her sleeping husband. God had visited her in this "ah ha" moment. The kaleidoscope had moved. She was seeing things in a different light, a light that would enable the whole family to grow.

All of us have experienced "ah ha" moments, moments when we have been struck by the insight, the answer, the newness of something. It might be an answer to an issue we have been debating for a long time, or an understanding of why another person acts the way he or she does, or a sudden deep appreciation of a butterfly or a sunset or another person. In these moments we truly feel that God is beside us, God's hand firmly in the moment, providing us with the insight that extends beyond the present into the creations that are yet to come.

Continuing Creation

Meister Eckhart, a thirteenth-century mystic, said, "God is creating the entire universe, fully and totally in the present now." Creation, all of creation, is a work-in-progress. That gives everyone of us a share in creation, and every work we do a work of art. The "ah ha" moments are the times when God reminds us to stay on course so that we all can work toward the fullness of creation.

Creativity is integral because it is life. None of us can run from it, none of us can claim not to have it, none of us can say it is only extra, the play of life. All of us need to step up and share our creativity if we want a better world, a better church. We have to place ourselves in the hands of the great Creator if we want to really find our life.

Something to Think About

- What do I imagine my birth was like?
- When I think of sharing creation with God, what feelings arise?
- How did my last "ah ha" moment make me more present to life?
- In what ways am I creative each day?
- What is my creative name for God?

CHAPTER 3

Obstacles to Creativity

Maybe it all began when Adam and Eve were banished from the Garden of Eden, or maybe it began with the invention of television or with instant communication. Whatever the reason, we have each day said goodbye to creativity, goodbye to life. The refrain of our time is, "I'm not creative."

When the creativity of preschool children is observed by their teachers, the imagination of the children is bubbling over at better than ninety-eight percent. Four or five years later, as children enter the second grade, their creativity level has dropped to four percent or less. Levels for adults subject to the same observation have been rated at one percent or less.

How staggering that in their early years these older children and adults were endlessly inquisitive. They used their mouths and eyes and hands to probe and analyze everything in order to make it part of their world. Their ability to learn languages was amazing when you realize that this achievement is not only linguistic but also scientific and philosophical. Just about every parent can vouch for the fact that once children reached this stage, their endless "why" questions on every conceivable topic became the rule of the day.

Somewhere between that magical time and the "grown-up" years, creativity dims and in some cases disappears entirely. We think this occurrence is very natural. After all, we reason, we're adults. We have to act responsibly. We have to limit our creativity to a hobby (if we have one) or to our choice of clothes and the houses we live in. Not bad, but still not the fullness of creation.

The fact remains that creativity is easier to stamp out than to build up. What is it that kills the creative life in us?

The Right and Wrong Answers

One of the biggest obstacles to the growth of creativity is what we call "the right answer." Too early and too often we are taught that there is only one right answer. Rarely is this the case. For many things and occasions in life there are second right answers and often third and fourth right ones. Because of our obsession with the right answer, educator Neil Postman says children enter school as question marks and leave as periods.

The right answer lies in drawing inside the lines. The right answer requires that we follow the formula for solving a problem. The right answer means mimicking or memorizing an answer to a religion question, a question that often doesn't have just one right or wrong answer. Is it wrong to answer the question "Why did God make you?" with "God made me to enjoy creation, to work with others to further creation and to enjoy it with God and others throughout this life and the next," instead of "to know God, to love God, and to serve God in this world and to be happy with God forever in the next"?

If we want our creative selves back, we have to realize that there are as many ways of answering questions as ways to turn the kaleidoscope. When we limit ourselves to only one approach to a solution, we limit our life and creativity. When we turn the kaleidoscope, we are able to see varied responses to the same question. This type of thinking enriches our lives and our understanding of God.

Keeping the Rules

Another obstacle to creativity is following rules. Before I am accused of promoting false or incorrect teaching, let me say that rules are good. They bring order to our lives. Without rules we would have no idea of what to do in certain situations. We know that at a traffic light people will stop on red, go on green, and generally exhibit caution on yellow. Rules keep us safe.

But imagine yourself on the road at 3 AM, with a very sick child in the car. You're on your way to the hospital, and you come to a traffic light. The signal is red and is known to be one of the longest lights in the area. What do you do? Do you look both ways and continue through the red light toward the hospital, or do you wait the three minutes for the light to change on a deserted street?

Sometimes rules have to be broken. Now here's a secret: many of the things we look upon as rules are not really rules at all. They are the "rules" that develop as a result of habitually doing things a certain way. All of us have encountered the cardinal rule entitled, "We've Always Done It This Way." This rule dictates certain actions in a great many situations, and usually no one knows how the rule began.

A story is told of a newly married wife who was cooking dinner for her husband, her parents, and her grandmother. She had decided on baking a ham. She pushed cloves into the ham, then proceeded to cut off the rounded portion. When her husband asked her why she was doing that, she replied that she had learned it from the way her mother cooked ham.

Curious, the husband asked his mother-in-law why she cut the ham that particular way. Was it to make the meat cook more evenly? Was it because the flavor was better? His mother-in-law shook her head and said, "That was how my mother always cooked ham."

"I see," he replied but still was not satisfied. He went to his wife's grandmother sitting in the living room and posed the question. "Your granddaughter and your daughter both said they learned how to cook ham from you. I would like to know why you cut off the rounded portion of the ham."

The older woman looked at him and smiled. "Well," she said, "if I remember correctly, the first ham we got was much too large for the stove in our apartment. The only way I could think of to cook it was to cut off the end so that it would fit into the oven."

Often the rules that spring from "We've Always Done It That Way" have some strange origins, as you can see from this story. We seldom question why we do something a particular way. We just accept it as the best way, as the rule. So we limit creativity.

What Will Other People Think?

Spontaneity is often a part of creativity. How many times, though, have you resisted acting spontaneously because of what others might say or think? We worry about whether or not we will be judged, whether what we do measures up to the ideas or expectations of those around us. This fear of what others will say limits our ability to create. We no longer think for ourselves but rather think as a group. We rely on the responses and behavior of the group to a particular event. When people fail to act spontaneously and instead follow what everyone else is doing, people become clones of one another, something that is never healthy.

As a result, individuals are chained to what they already know. They will often remain only in their field of expertise and never venture beyond it into another field. Crossing over into other fields of knowledge is very important to creativity. Specialists need to take advantage of experiences outside of their frame of reference if they want to grow in their own field and if they want to discover new things. We wouldn't have roll-on deodorant if a scientist hadn't observed how ball point pens glide. Knute Rockne's four horsemen backfield shift resulted from watching a burlesque chorus routine.

When we worry about what other people will think, we don't dare cross over into new fields. We don't allow ourselves to explore, to take risks. We create invisible boundaries that we dare not cross. That invisible boundary keeps creativity reined in.

Clowns are "fools" who don't worry about what people think. "We are fools for Christ's sake," says Paul when speaking to the Corinthians, and he takes that literally. When we are fully creative, we are willing to be clowns for Christ, no matter what people think or say.

The Too Late, Too Old, Play-Is-for-Kids Syndrome

Often during the course of growing up we are told to act our age, or to act in a mature way, or to be adult. These words are sure to kill creativity because creativity needs play to grow. Surprise, surprise! Play is okay no matter what your age.

How many times have you seen children playing while an adult or adults are in close proximity? What are the children doing? What are the adults doing? Odds are that the children are pretending to be pirates or astronauts or experimenting with how the sand falls through the cracks of the swing. The adults, instead, are talking or just sitting and watching. When we do see an adult playing with children, often our first thought is how strange that is, or we become concerned that the adults might be planning a kidnapping! When we see an adult in a grocery store singing or dancing down the aisles, do we accept that as a playful moment, or do we wonder what is wrong with that person? We wonder why they don't act their age.

Play is crucial to creativity. Play relaxes the mind and opens it up to ideas. Play enables us to combine different ideas and try them out. During play our defenses are down and all the mental limits we put on ourselves vanish. When we play, we forget about rules and being practical and being wrong. We just enjoy ourselves and our world.

As for being too old or too late, both of those arguments are motivated by pride. If we play, we are afraid of looking silly or stupid or unsophisticated. When we swallow our pride, we are able to play and allow creativity to flow.

An old Polish grandma would often pull candy out of unsuspecting people's ears, eliciting a smile from the other person. A young teen in our neighborhood makes origami cranes and leaves them on the table when he finishes eating at restaurants, bringing exclamations of delight from the servers. The real trick is that he uses whatever material is at hand—napkins, fast food wrappers, newspapers. My 94-year-old grandfather would dance on the sidewalk just for the fun of it. After his death, the neighbors realized the joy this man brought when he played.

Play doesn't have to be complicated and doesn't have to involve playground equipment or toys. Play is our ability to let loose and enjoy the world around us in whatever expression we choose. Doing so stokes our creativity and therefore enriches our lives. We are never too old, never too late to play. When we allow it to happen, we share in co-creation.

I Am Not Creative

The biggest obstacle to co-creation is believing we are not creative. This is one of the greatest self-fulfilling prophecies that keep us from realizing our potential as sons and daughters of God, as co-creators, as having been created in the image of God. Whenever we say we are not creative it is an insult to God. God created us in his image and likeness and we are to bring that image and likeness to each other. That image is the ability to create with God, to realize the fullness of life, to love with our whole being.

Our ability to create comes from an Eternal Wonder. When we use that ability, we move toward our God. Each time we claim we are not creative, we turn our backs on that ability, on the opportunity to discover what we are really capable of. Our lack of belief in our creativity limits us, and consequently we lose the fullness of life.

Hope

The fullness of life is all around us. For many reasons we have fallen away from recognizing that fullness and we have squashed our ability to share in God's creation. However, if we cultivate our creativity, we will open ourselves more and more to that abundance. We might encounter obstacles on our paths. We have seen some of them. But the most encouraging reality is that we can employ many ways to resurrect or nurture our creativity. It all starts with baby steps.

Something to Think About

- When do I feel there is only one right answer to something?
- When have I been wrong about that answer?
- When has following the rules caused me trouble?
- What value is there to breaking certain rules?
- When was the last time I played?
- What value does play have to our community?
- What other ways have I or the community blocked creativity?

CHAPTER 4

Everything Has a Purpose

"Okay! Whose turn was it to clean up the mess this time?" Noah's wife screeched the words. Elephant dung seeped up between her toes. "How many times?..." Her face reddened, and she found it impossible to get out the rest of the words.

Noah rushed over to her, abandoning his efforts to get more hay into the camels' food bin. He grabbed his wife. "Leah, Leah. Settle down. It's only dung. It can't hurt you." Noah pulled off his towel. "Sit down, will you, and I'll clean this up." He tried to clean the still-squirming toes.

Suddenly with a plop Leah came down on a cross plank that separated the stalls. Noah continued to clean the now silent Leah. The air was ominous. Then like a rain cloud finally reaching the point of saturation, Leah broke into tears.

"I can't take any more of this. Dung in my hair, on my feet, in my food. When is this going to end?"

"Now, now, dear." Noah awkwardly patted her shoulder. "Only a few more days."

"A few more days?" she exploded. "It's already been twenty-seven days! I can't take any more." The crash of thunder punctuated her statements.

Leah glared at Noah. "God could not have created dung!" she shouted.

"Now, now, dear. God knows what to do. There must be a purpose for it. We just have to wait and see what emerges."

"What emerges?" hurumphed Leah. "What emerges is a great big pile of dung."

Finding the Purpose

Later that afternoon, Leah worked on the upper deck of the ark. Most of the animals had settled down for their afternoon nap. Leah should have been taking one too because it was the only sleep she would get. Most of the animals stayed up all night, braying and cackling and roaring. But she couldn't sleep. The morning encounter with dung had played havoc on her nerves.

She pushed open the huge door to the garden room. The plants were doing so poorly, what with little sun and way too much rain. The small tomatoes and the pitiful beans would barely supply the vitamins the family needed to stay healthy. The vegetables needed all the help they could get. Leah also noticed there was only half the soil they had when they had started out in the ark. Anyway, thought Leah, we have to do something or we are not going to survive. She tucked a stray wisp of hair back into her head kerchief. As she did so, some bird dung fell from her head.

She jumped back, surveying the pieces on the floor with disgust. There it was again. What was she going to do with it all? The droppings certainly seemed to blend in with the soil quite well. They even looked like they belonged there. She picked up the droppings and worked them into the soil around a bean plant. There, she thought, the soil looks a little fuller.

The rest of the day was spent doing all the chores necessary to keep the ark running smoothly. The animals were all fed, the family had eaten, and all the repairs had been done for the day. As the moon rose, the family settled into prayer and conversation, until finally they were ready for sleep. Leah was surprised that, despite the sounds of the animals around her, she fell into a deep, dreamless sleep.

A Discovery

The dawn brought a new day and another list of chores and more rain. Leah found herself once again back at the garden room, hoping to gather enough vegetables for a stew. The wind had picked up, the air had chilled, and a stew sounded warm and comforting.

In the garden the first thing she saw was the bean plant that had received her gift of dung. Leah rubbed her eyes to make sure she wasn't dreaming. The plant was a full foot taller than the others around it, and it didn't have only three or four beans but at least twenty. Was it possible that the dung was good for something and wasn't just an annoyance? She fingered the soil. Somehow it seemed stronger and more porous.

"Noah! Come quickly!"

"Not again," she heard him moan from around the corner.

Leah smiled at Noah as he came through the door, towel in hand. He stopped in his tracks. She held out some of the soil. "Look at this, Noah."

He eyed her suspiciously, wondering if this was going to be payback for the elephant's "gift" yesterday.

"Oh, Noah! I just want you to see what happened to the plant. I added dung to the soil yesterday. The plant has lots of new flowers and over twenty bean pods. The dung must have made the difference." The excitement of her discovery was making her face rosy.

Noah bent and examined the plant carefully. He, too, was amazed at the difference.

"Why, Leah, I do believe you discovered something here. The dung must contain just the boost the plants need. Maybe there are vitamins and minerals in the stuff that plants like, even if we don't."

Leah nodded in agreement. "Exactly what I was thinking." She looked across the room. "I think our work this afternoon will be mostly in here. We are going to mix different types of dung into the soil and see what happens. We'll have our crop no matter what. The results may be small and measly or tall and abundant." She turned and smiled at Noah. "And if this works, you'll never hear me complain about dung again."

And God and Noah and Leah saw that what they had done was very good and there was evening and morning on the one hundredth and twelfth day.

CHAPTER 5

Opening the Door to Creation

Creativity is not something new. The creative spirit has manifested itself in various ways, in every person over the years. Once an individual says yes to life, yes to joining God in creation, life is no longer the same. Things happen, understanding deepens, and the sphere of possibilities expands.

When we talk about getting back in touch with our ability to share in creation with God, we have to acknowledge that when we choose creation, we choose to be different because the very essence of creation is uniqueness. In a society that prizes uniformity, this trait is not always appreciated. When, however, individuals are able to accept this important pre-requisite of creativity, they are able to free themselves to be open to the work of the Spirit in their lives. It is helpful to remember all those who have gone before us, using the gift of the Creator, alive in the Spirit—all those who accepted being different as an important first step to allowing God's creative power to shine through them.

First and Foremost

Jesus is the model for all creative actions. From the moment of his birth, he was different. Though a king, he was born in a stable instead of a rich palace. A leader, he chose to live in a small town with his parents, listening and learning until it was time to speak. As a healer, he didn't use the accepted ostentatious rituals of the day. Instead, he made mud packs to restore sight and drew in the sand to offer spiritual healing. Jesus was different, and in that, he was able to find the fullness of his mission. He allowed his Father to work through him. He could answer his mother when it wasn't "cool" to answer the demands of a nagging parent. Jesus was able to use his gifts because he was willing to be himself, to recognize his uniqueness and to respond accordingly.

How often have we tried to imitate someone else, hoping we could have their gifts? How often have we tried to be someone other than ourselves because we were worried about what people might think? How often have we sacrificed our uniqueness rather than stand out in a crowd? Jesus was willing to use his gifts. He didn't worry about what the Pharisees or the Roman soldiers thought of him. He was willing to be himself regardless of the rules he was supposed to follow. Jesus followed in the footsteps of his Father, the Creator, by using his ability to create, to bring life, whenever and wherever he had the chance.

Not Afraid to Be Different

People throughout the ages have worked with their Creator, seeking out their uniqueness and sharing it with others. Sister Thea Bowman is a good example of how a person's gifts and efforts blossom when he or she works with the Creator.

Of African-American heritage, Sister Thea entered the Franciscan Sisters of Perpetual Adoration, having been attracted to the order during her school years. She didn't blend in, though, because for her it was important that her African-American background be part of her spirituality. She was not afraid of being ridiculed or rejected.

Sister Thea was noted for her presentations, which included spirituals and stories. She challenged the people listening to go out and live and preach the gospel with enthusiasm. Often her audiences would be surprised to find themselves participating through singing and comments and prayer.

When Sister Thea was diagnosed with breast cancer, she continued to make presentations, which were now filled with poignancy and faith. She would often say that her prayer during her illness was a simple one: Lord, let me live until I die.

This woman realized that she was creating with God, she was calling people to the fullness of faith, and she was a living creation creating for others. She wasn't afraid of being different.

Dom Virgil Michel was another person who was willing to risk the consequences of following his Creator. A monk of St. John's Abbey in Collegeville, Minnesota, he found ways to look for the ever-changing newness of creation. Dom Michel was intensely interested in the liturgical movement, but he was troubled by the passive mode of the participants at Mass. At that time (the 1930s) Mass was in Latin, and the priest faced away from the people. Often the Mass seemed more like a private prayer between the priest and God, with the people as mere observers.

By being open to the Spirit, Dom Michel saw the importance of once again emphasizing that the Mass is the central expression of the living church. Well before the Second Vatican Council, he was advocating the teaching about the mystical body of Christ. He also supported the movement away from a faith community in which clergy were considered to be more spiritual than the common person. He felt strongly that the witness of the Christian was intimately connected to the quality of the worship service. Dom Michel believed in the role of the laity and that their witness in the daily routine of their lives is a way of holiness. He recognized the power that routine had to enhance creativity. Because he was willing to be different, he was able to prepare other people for the sweeping changes that Vatican II would bring. His courage in following his gifts enabled him to be a messenger for his Creator.

Being Open to Creativity

Francis Xavier is another prime example of being open to creativity. Around 1530, he left home to study at the University of Paris. There he met Ignatius of Loyola. The two became fast friends, and together with six other men they formed the Society of Jesus. All of them believed they were called to bring the news of Jesus to all people.

Francis' first mission took him to India. He was surprised to find that those who had preceded him had indeed shared Christianity with the natives; however, they had believed that the dark-skinned people were less in the eyes of God than the light-skinned preachers. This saddened Francis greatly. He wondered what he could do to help people come to Christ within their own culture. He didn't hesitate to ask God for help, and he wasn't disappointed. An idea came to him. He would live as one of them. He learned their language, dressed as they did, slept as they slept. Francis traveled all over India in this manner, becoming one with the people, spreading the good news of Jesus. People came to love him and to know him as the person with a God who loved the poor and who gave them new life.

Francis listened to God and shared in creation with God as he developed the idea of service within the culture of the people. All this happened because he was willing to be different when he decided to dress and live in the same way as the people he served.

Ambrose is another saint open to God creating through him. Ambrose, too, was willing to be different. As Bishop of Milan, Italy, he felt he should always speak his mind as well as call people to account for their actions. For example, when the emperor of the time allowed soldiers to kill innocent people, Ambrose demanded that the emperor ask for forgiveness. When the Roman governor allowed people to worship false gods in a local church, Ambrose confronted them in a unique way. He called the people together, and they sat in the church singing, praying and staying, refusing to move until the churches were acknowledged to be sacred places for the Christians. Ambrose was open to the gift of creating with God. He was able to develop a way of dealing with the situations he faced in a unique and positive manner.

A person with a very different lifestyle who responded to the Creator's gift was Rahab, the prostitute (see Joshua, chapter two). She offered shelter in her house, which abutted the city wall, to two of Joshua's spies. When the king of the city insisted she turn over the spies, she hid them instead, after securing her safety and her refuge with their God. She saw that the God of Israel was full of power, and she was willing to follow that God no matter what was required, even at the risk of being different. Joshua honored the promise the two spies had made to her, and she lived out the rest of her days with the people of Israel.

Being Comfortable with Being Different

The list of people who were and are willing to be different so that they can work with God in the continuation of creation is long. Housewives and lawyers, dancers and missionaries, teachers and doctors, children and elderly, and many others are on this list. People of all shapes and sizes, each willing to be unique so they might know the fullness of creation.

It's not always comfortable to feel we are not the same as other persons. I know that first hand. Because my marriage to Ed was a flower-child marriage, he and I were very eclectic in our choice of furnishings and the decoration of our living quarters. Our first apartment sported posters proclaiming our stance against the Viet Nam war. In our bedroom, a large apple tree was painted on one wall with one apple hanging from it. One day I added the story to the wall for all to see. The story was of a man who planted the apple tree and who, harvest after harvest, found it without apples. The owner decided to cut it down. When he came to the orchard, armed with an axe, he found an apple on the tree. The message on that wall was to assure those who saw it that the fruits would come. They would come despite outward appearances to the contrary. We carried this moral into our other apartments and houses.

In Marfa, Texas, we lived in an old adobe house where the toilet was on one end of the house and the rest of the bathroom on another. How many laughs we enjoyed when unsuspecting visitors went into the bathroom only to find no toilet! In Minnesota, we became the owners of a large telephone spool which, after we cleaned and sanded it, became our dining room table. Many a meal was shared around it, and when we moved to Kansas, we took it with us. Today, twenty-five years later, the table is still in our living room, a reminder to us not only of good friends and family but also of the call to be comfortable with being different.

It wasn't always that way. When we first arrived in Johnson County, Kansas, that county was one of the most affluent in the United States. Our house was small but cozy. In addition to our telephone spool table, we had a lobster trap coffee table, a church pew in our living room, wicker baskets as lampshades, and books all over the place.

One particular evening we were to have a meeting with a group of teenagers in order to plan an upcoming event. I had been in some of their houses, and our house could comfortably fit into their living rooms. When the youth arrived, I remember thinking how small our living room had suddenly become. I watched as some of the kids shifted uncomfortably on the pew. I saw them smile politely at our table. And we even got a "what's that ugly thing?" about our lobster trap. I felt increasingly uncomfortable. I was unable to join in the meeting.

That night, I shared my thoughts with Ed. We talked for a long time. I realized that I liked our lobster trap—and it fulfilled a lifelong dream of Ed's to be able to put his feet up on the coffee table. I loved our spool table. We were able to seat a large number of people around it. I had to face the fact that my tastes were my tastes, my interests were my interests. That day I learned that I need to be comfortable with who I am and with being different, even when people around me hint at or even verbalize their disapproval.

Dealing with the Fear

When we are challenged to be true to ourselves, true to our call to share in God's creative power, we find that we are of necessity unique because God has created each of us as individuals. Our biggest challenge in living our uniqueness is fear. Fear rears its ugly head time and time again whenever we try to make the leap into creativity.

We fear being laughed at, a fear that springs out of insecurity. This basic fear can tie our hands when we attempt to answer God's call. We don't trust our own abilities. We don't want to be ridiculed for making a mistake. This fear hinders us from sharing our abilities because we might be laughed at. Would that we grow to the point where we worry, instead, about what God will think if we don't use our gifts for ourselves and others!

Another obstacle that crops up when we feel called to take the leap into creativity is our worry about the unknown. Such worry prevents us from using our creative ability and from being ourselves. Consider for a moment what life would be like today had the early settlers been paralyzed by the fear of the unknown. Any land west of the Appalachians might very well still be wild country. The pioneers had to travel long, difficult distances, encountering dangers they had not even imagined. Those of us who have come after them can enjoy that large expanse of land.

In order to be comfortable with being ourselves—the very first requisite of creativity—we have to learn to live with the unknown, with uncertainty. Our faith in God will carry us where we need to be and help us in creative moments to adapt, react, and grow.

Fear of rejection and of revealing our true selves can manifest itself when we attempt to turn the kaleidoscope in order to recognize our creative potential. We are afraid of failing and forget the times when we failed and began again until we learned whatever we needed to—whether it was learning to walk, or write, or dance. Worse still, we may doubt ourselves and be apprehensive that people may find out that we cannot do what we claim we can. We dread having our true selves revealed.

What groundless fears! If others see us as we are, they will find persons who share in God's creative action—as they do. Our heavenly Father calls us to create each day, using the unique gifts that he gives to each one of us.

When I was recovering from alcoholism, I repeated for the umpteenth time at one of our meetings my fears about being able to stay sober and the new life that was opening to me. One of the women looked at me and said, "You do know that fear is an insult to God. God wants us to trust that he loves us more than we will ever know."

Come, trust our God and join all the people who have chosen to follow their Creator, who feel comfortable in being unique, who are willing to take the leap so they might grow in their creativity, in their very life.

Something to Think About

- At what times in my life have I felt different from the world around me?
- What is my biggest fear when I look to being creative?
- When do I fail to trust God?
- Whom have I seen as someone who is comfortable with being themselves?
- How are Christians called to be different?
- How is remembering my call to share in creation going to change my life? How has it already changed it?

CHAPTER 6

Beginnings and Middles

Once we are ready to take our rightful place as co-creators with God and once we are ready to trust God to guide us in this endeavor, there are different ways in which we can cultivate life and creativity.

One of the most important elements toward becoming aware of creativity is the cultivation of a beginner's mind. When you cultivate a beginner's mind you begin to look at yourself, the others around you, and the whole world as always new.

Picture yourself at home in your living room. Outside the window in plain sight is a river, which flows out into the sea day after day, without stopping, without changing. However, when you begin to look at the river from a different viewpoint, you find that such is not the truth.

The river is changing constantly. The water is ever new, coming from upstream and finding its way to this place, at this moment. The water is sometimes clear, sometimes cloudy, sometimes warm to the touch, sometimes freezing. It is populated by various creatures at distinct times of the year. A water snake darts along, fighting the current. Tiny tadpoles swim frantically, growing quickly into frogs. Even the organisms we cannot see change. The bacteria in the water grow or diminish according to a number of factors—

the heat, the presence of chemicals upstream, the animals who come to quench their thirst. The molecules keep dividing and changing as the water moves along on its journey toward the sea. The river is ever new, if we only look.

We might also consider a toddler. Look at her life on the surface: the toddler arises in the morning, doing many of the things that go into a day—eating, sleeping, talking, playing. However, if we reflect more deeply, a toddler is and does so much more. How the child eats breakfast one day differs from the day before. She notices that the taste of the juice is not the same and wonders why. At playtime, she finds new and different uses for a very old toy. Her toy rabbit becomes a dragon, a house, or her baby. The toddler checks out the world upside down and sideways, always discovering something new and interesting. When she climbs into bed, she is a different person from the child who awoke in the morning. She may look the same but her engagement with creation has changed her for the better.

Insight

That's what a beginner's mind does—it looks at the world as ever new, ever ready for new creations. We look at the world as ever new, ever ready for unexplored creations. God gives us this spark to collect ideas, to examine them closely, to mix them together and see which ones are compatible. This spark enables us to bring fresh ideas, untried thoughts, and remarkable things to life.

Osho, one of the most provocative spiritual teachers of the twentieth century, said, "A creative person is one who has insight, who can see things nobody else has ever seen before, who hears things that nobody has heard before." The presence of God in us enables us to see the river ever-new. It helps the toddler discover so much each day. It enables us to be co-creators if only we can turn the kaleidoscope and observe life from an original perspective.

When we consider the world with a beginner's mind, we are not afraid to ask questions. We want to know as much as we can about whatever it is we are dealing with. In the liturgy and in religion sessions we hear the same Scripture readings and the same teachings over and over again, particularly if we are cradle Catholics. Unfortunately this fact might create in us a "heard it, know it" way of thinking.

The Prodigal Son

For example, because we have heard the story of the prodigal son time and again, we think we know it. We know about the father and how the boy took his inheritance and squandered it and then had to work with the pigs that had more food than he did. On reflection, the son returns to his father, asking forgiveness for what he has done. The father welcomes the son with open arms even before the son can ask for forgiveness. That's the story. Nothing more. Nothing less.

With a beginner's mind, we are able to look at the story as if we had first discovered it. We listen to the words once again. "There was a man who had two sons..." and we hear things we didn't hear the first time. Light bulbs begin to switch on.

Ah, he had two sons. What happened to the other son while the prodigal son was off gambling? Had the prodigal son met anyone who questioned why he was squandering the money? If he had, how might his life be different? Did the father have to deal with his urge to go and find his son and make sure he was safe? How did the other son feel, with the father so preoccupied about his lost son? Did the prodigal son question the father's welcome? And once the son had settled back into the routine of life, did he have an urge to leave again? All these questions and more would arise in the beginner's mind. And soon those questions would spark other questions. A beginner's mind would always be looking for more, moving the kaleidoscope and seeing things in a new way.

Recently I had the opportunity to work with parents and their children as they prepared for the sacrament of reconciliation. Within the program we talked about what different passages in Scripture say about forgiveness. All the passages were stories we had heard many times before. However, we approached them in very different ways.

We acted out the parable of the lost sheep, with one father hunting throughout the church for the one lost sheep, while the other sheep huddled together for warmth.

We set the prodigal son story to music, each group giving a very different interpretation of the songs necessary for the various parts of the parable. Everyone said these two experiences had helped them look at these Scripture passages in a totally different way. Each person had put on a beginner's mind while doing this simple exercise.

Discovery

Another easy first step in developing your creativity is to cultivate an approach of exploration and discovery. Focus on specific topics you don't know. Look at them closely and ask the questions that come to mind. Play around with whatever you are working on and be curious. Imagine yourself as coming into the situation as into a totally new environment, like an alien, perhaps, from another planet who knows nothing of our life and culture. Or look at these topics from the perspective of a different world culture. What distinctions would come to light? Keep your outlook fresh, and examine everything with an open mind, and you will find that your creative spirit begins to grow.

A religious educator had to do a presentation to families about preparing their children for their First Eucharist. She didn't want the families to look at the session as "been there, done that." Instead she wanted them to walk away with a new insight into what Eucharist was for them so that they could share their beliefs with their children.

The first thing the educator did was to imagine that she had never done the presentation before. She tried to imagine what it would be like to know nothing about the Eucharist.

First she thought about bread. What was bread? The staff of life, the one food necessary for life. What you had around the house after everything else was eaten. So, she thought, bread is essential. Bread is the food that connects us with past generations. Bread is universal.

But, her train of thought continued, so few people today know what goes into the making of bread. Lots of hard work. The harvest, the grinding, the preparing of ingredients. And as this thought process continued, as she tried to look at things in a new way and to imagine herself ready to share the Eucharist with a group of "aliens," she came up with unique ways to do so. The parents at that gathering ground wheat into flour; mixed the ingredients, each of which was labeled with an aspect of faith; kneaded the dough; waited while it rose—a contemplation on resurrection and new life that kept them focused; then baked the bread and ate it. The result was that their understanding of the Eucharist was deepened, they were able to ponder what they believed, and the activity consequently enhanced the preparation of their children.

One of the main things this educator did during the process was to seek new ideas from many different sources. While she was imagining that she was addressing an alien group, she read and looked into and asked about various approaches. And each time she searched for ideas, she checked to make sure that they were fresh, that she wasn't falling back on things she had done before.

Connections

Based on what you know about both of them, what do you suppose would happen if King David met George Bush? What type of interchange do you suppose they would have? Or what connection would the word "growler" have with Jesus meeting the Pharisees?

These questions might yield interesting and creative approaches to a particular subject.

Connections are an integral part of opening yourself to creativity. Connections enable you to look into another area for an original approach. Most of us are familiar with the task of the bee that flies from flower to flower, collecting the nectar and, at the same time, pollinating the plants. Without this work, plants would have a difficult time producing their fruit. Through the bees' work, however, the plant yields the fruit we are able to enjoy. The same principle applies to creativity. When you cross-fertilize, when you make connections between objects and realities, you open the door to unexplored ideas and creative thought.

When you put together two people who come from totally different backgrounds, you discover things you might not otherwise have thought about. Perhaps King David would ask George Bush what he found most difficult about his job as president. Perhaps David would talk about his leadership of the people of Israel. George Bush might ask David how he felt about war.

When you choose words at random from the dictionary and connect them with a person or concept, interesting things result. The word "growler" has a few definitions. A growler is a being, such as a dog, who growls. A growler is also a small iceberg, as well as a container for carrying beer. Lastly, a growler is an electromagnetic device with two poles used for magnetizing, demagnetizing, and finding short-circuited coil. When this word is connected to the Pharisees, it raises some interesting thoughts. For example, using the iceberg definition, what lay under the surface for the Pharisees? Was this seen by people other than Jesus? Was Jesus the "electromagnetic device" that was able to find where the Pharisees were short-circuiting their faith? Could we take it a step further by asking ourselves who the "growlers" are in our lives, the persons who react in an angry and surly manner? How do we respond to them? Are we ourselves growlers?

Connections as simple as these yield a wealth of reflections and opportunities for growth in faith.

Another beautiful effect of connections is that we are able to better integrate our faith into our daily lives. Imagine I have asked you to make a connection between peanut butter and God. You might respond by saying that like peanut butter, God sticks with you. Or, since peanut butter is a staple in our lives, so too God should be a staple in our lives. The list could go on. The beauty of connections is that once you make them, they become a part of your life. Once you have made a connection between God and peanut butter, the next time you make a peanut butter sandwich, you will think of God. The same thing happens whenever you make a connection. When you draw a comparison between a chair and God, you can't sit in the chair without thinking of God. When you connect the attributes of a pencil to God, every word you write with it becomes infused with the Eternal Wonder. Connections are the lifeblood of creativity.

Connections not only enable us to get the creative juices flowing, they empower us to deepen our faith as we become more aware of God working in our lives in great and small ways. When you join or relate or connect ideas and people, you are inspired to new realms within your faith.

Learning to Play

Jesus knew what he was talking about when he exhorted his followers to become like little children. Children play, children open themselves up to learning. Children are not caught up in what they are supposed to do. We are often surrounded by people who get after us to "stop fooling around and get to work." Consequently our ability to create and celebrate life is hindered.

Play is the fertile ground of new ideas. When you are playing, you are not putting up walls to block out ideas or worrying that you might be wrong. You are just playing with your defenses down and your mind open to the Spirit. You are able to laugh at yourself.

Nowhere in Scripture does it say that Jesus laughed. My take on that is that the writers of Scripture were so intent on making sure the message was there that they became very serious, considering the message as something not to be taken lightly. But in a sense, Scripture is to be taken lightly because the message of Jesus calls us to love and love always lightens our burdens. Love makes life in its darkest moments bearable.

The movie *Life Is Beautiful* addressed just that subject. In the midst of the concentration camp's horrors, the father of a young boy was able to help everyone keep their spirits focused on the good of life, rather than on their present difficult situation. Through humor he was able to remind them that God is love, God is in control, and God would triumph. Humor reminds us that God loves us, and in a topsy-turvy world God rejoices in us always. Because of all this, I believe Jesus laughed and had a beautiful sense of humor.

Play and humor have a way of stretching our thinking. Whenever we appreciate a joke, it stretches our way of thinking. If John the Baptist and Winnie the Pooh can share the same middle name, what does that say about how we are alike and different? What does it say about combining ideas? If we see a bit of saint in every sinner, what does that say about our ability to see God in everyone?

When we allow ourselves to play, when we allow ourselves to laugh, we open the door wider to creativity. We will find that there is a short journey between the "ha-ha" of humor and the "ah-ha" of discovery.

Trusting the Spirit

It's hard. It's scary. It's the unknown. Trusting the Spirit can be a heart-stopping experience. Trusting the Spirit, though, is the most important thing we must do if we are serious about following our call to be co-creators with God.

We often talk about trusting the Spirit. We use words like "I'll go where the Spirit takes me," or "the Spirit's behind everything I do." But if we really mean those words, we are literally taking a leap. We are taking a leap from our comfortable in-control position in life to a place of unknown, surprising, and sometimes scary occurrences. We are open to whatever the Spirit sends, even if that means changing our usual approach to teaching or parenting or praying. We take the leap, and we join with the Creator and the Spirit to do things that bring the kingdom even closer to the people in our world.

The first time I remember really trusting the Spirit, I was terrified. My strategy was in my back pocket. The presentation on creativity was to a group of catechists at a state conference in Kansas. I was really looking forward to the program, since I had had a great deal of fun in preparing it. Once I saw all the people, it seemed that nothing I had prepared would work. But I was determined to go ahead with it.

And then, even before the session began, the Spirit started to work. My notes had disappeared. Frantically I wrote down what I could remember, trying to put my thoughts in an orderly fashion. But I ran out of time and I had no place to go except before this large group of catechists. "Oh, God, you said you would send your Spirit," I prayed, "and I need your Spirit now. I have no place to turn but to you." Suddenly I realized that I was no longer in control. What people call "flow" took over—a phenomenon that occurs when you no longer are thinking or worrying or wondering, but rather just being and allowing the material to "flow." The Spirit took over that day. The program turned out to be one of the most enriching I have ever experienced. I shared in the gift of creating with God because I had trusted the Spirit to take over. The biggest factor, which had been lacking in so many past presentations, was now present. God the Creator and Spirit empowered me to spread the good news of the kingdom.

Taking the leap to creativity, training ourselves to be open to life can be frightening, difficult, and full of unknowns, but it is so satisfying, freeing, and surprising. We learn that, as we trust in the Spirit, as we are open to creativity and to life, many gentle and powerful changes can take place in our lives. We just have to say "yes."

Something to Think About

- When am I most in touch with my creativity?
- What was the last thing I looked at with a beginner's mind?
- How does a beginner's mind change what I see?
- When I look at a person with a beginner's mind what happens?
- What discoveries have I made recently in my life?
- When have I trusted the Spirit?
- What does it mean to trust?

CHAPTER 7

The Lord Is with Us

The fire burned briskly, clouds of smoke dancing around the people. The campsite was alive with activity. People scurried around. They packed herbs and clothes and pottery. They made sure all their belongings were secure and ready for the morning. Tomorrow they would actually set foot in the Promised Land after so much time in the desert. Tomorrow they would be home.

As activity died down and people headed to bed, a small group of persons huddled by the fire. The group included Eleazar, a husky man whose eyes still showed his grief over the deaths of his father, Aaron, and his uncle Moses. Eleazar was now the high priest of the Israelites, and he didn't know if he was as capable as his father and uncle had been. He clenched his teeth, and felt his fists tightening. What if he failed?

His best friend, Abdi, knew the signs. Eleazar had forgotten that God was in charge.

"Good friend," he said to Eleazar, "you fail to trust again."

Eleazar looked at him in surprise. Abdi nodded toward the clenched fists.

"You fail to trust the Lord, who has gotten us through so much."

Eleazar smiled weakly at his friend. "You know me too well." He took up a long stick and poked at the embers, stoking a flame. Tears filled his eyes. "It is so frightening. I am to lead these people into the Promised Land tomorrow, and I am afraid." He looked at Abdi. "I don't know what I am supposed to do. What will happen if we meet with soldiers who do not see us as people come to settle in a new land? How long will the people follow me? You know how they reacted to my father and my uncle."

Abdi took Eleazar's hand in his. "I don't know the answers to your questions. But I do know that the Lord has been with us. I do know what happened when we trusted the Lord, when we worked with the Holy One."

Eleazar stared blankly at Abdi, seeing in his mind's eye only the unknown. He jumped when Abdi snapped his fingers.

"I think it is time we took a journey back."

"What?" Eleazar gave a start, shocked that his friend was suggesting a journey back into the desert, a desert that has been so hard on them.

Abdi laughed. "No, I don't mean to journey with our camels and belongings back toward that harsh land. I mean that we should remember what the journey was like."

Eleazar shook his head. "I don't know if I want to go back. It will be too painful."

"Then it is even more important to go back because you have forgotten the joy."

Memories

Abdi moved closer to the campfire, reached for some twigs, and added them to the coals.

"Let us start at the beginning. Remember the Red Sea?"

"Do I remember it?" Eleazar laughed scornfully. "I was fifteen and I thought my heart would leap from my chest. Not only were the Egyptians after us, but those walls of water threatened to come down on us at any time. And even though we walked on dry land, my clothes were soaked by the time we reached the other side."

"Are you sure it wasn't your sweat that made them so wet?" Abdi's eyes twinkled. "I remember you were so scared I had to run to keep up with you, you were moving so fast."

Eleazar smiled at the memory. "That was pretty great, though. To think that our God could do such a feat!"

"Don't forget the help the Holy One received."

"What? The Lord didn't need help."

Moses

"True, the Lord didn't need help, but he wanted it. The Lord asked for Moses to lift up his staff and part the waters. If Moses hadn't done that, the waters wouldn't have parted. Do you think we would have ventured into the water, even if it were parted, especially if we just saw it suddenly part on its own? We would have been really worried that it was a trick of the Pharaoh. Instead, Moses worked with the Lord and parted the sea so all of us could trust." Abdi paused. "Well, all of us except you!"

Eleazar playfully kicked a few embers toward Abdi. "Seems I recall a time when you weren't Mr. Brave Fellow. Remember when we encountered the Amalekites? You were afraid that would be the end of us all. Although you fought bravely, you didn't think the battle would be won."

Abdi nodded his head, recalling to mind the fierce battles. The fear rose in him again.

"You had forgotten that Moses and Aaron were once again working with God to bring a resolution to the conflict. Remember how Moses held the rod of God aloft? As long as he did so, we kept the upper hand. When Moses got tired, Aaron and Nadab helped to hold his arms aloft." Eleazar looked toward the heavens. "We were victorious that day and were able to continue our journey toward this Promised Land."

"Eleazar, you remind me well about the times I have failed to trust, to work with our God."

Eleazar continued to study the stars, watching their brightness against an ebony sky. "But remember, Abdi, that you were the one brave enough to believe the gift that had come to us from God, the day we almost went our separate ways, tired and hungry and discouraged."

Abdi coughed. "That wasn't anything great. You would have done it too."

"Maybe, but we only know that you did it and saved our people."

"Hey, I was hungry. We had asked for food the night before, and so I guessed this was what we had been given to eat." He brought out a piece of bread from his pouch. "And it was a lot better than this." He looked quickly around. "Not that my wife doesn't make good bread, you know. The manna. You know. It was heavenly."

Eleazar chuckled. "Especially when you made that stack of manna and poured honey over it. I had to laugh at the number of people who tried the same thing!"

"It was good, though. I hadn't tasted something that good in a long time. How long had we been in the desert then?"

"About fifteen years. A lot of the older people who had seen the miracle of the water had died. Perhaps the Lord figured that we needed another burst of power." He looked back to Abdi. "And the Lord gave it to us. You helped the Lord when you just plunged right in and ate the manna, creating all sorts of new delicacies with it. I'll never forget that picture of you smiling, with honey dripping from your mouth and manna held high in your hands. Such a great God."

Do Not Be Afraid

"Don't forget the quail and the water and all the little surprises along the way." Abdi's voice took on a serious quality. "And that, my friend, is why you shouldn't be afraid. The Lord will be with us always. We just have to be willing to work with the Lord, not forgetting, always trusting." He paused. "Remember what happened when your uncle went up Mt. Sinai and he was gone for what seemed like forever? Remember how we all lost trust that he would return, that the Lord would take care of us?"

Abdi choked with emotion, anger erupting. "We didn't trust the Lord. Instead we put our trust in a small gold cow. We worshiped it." He shook his head in disbelief. "How could we have been so stupid? How could we have done such a thing after everything the Lord did with and for us?"

"We forget, Abdi, about the Lord's constant love for us. We forget how the Lord is always ready to work alongside us if we are willing to work and walk alongside the Lord."

"Ah, my friend, you fear no more. I can see our talk has had good results." Abdi looked to the heavens. "And I predict, because you are willing to work with the Lord, that scandal shall not plague you, that you shall be most loyal and generous, serving well as priest." His face lit up in a smile. "And when you come to allot portions of the Promised Land, I know you will give an especially fertile and large one to me." Abdi winked.

Eleazar grabbed his friend in a warm embrace. "Only if God agrees."

And God and Eleazar and Abdi saw that everything was good and there was evening and morning on the forty-four thousand, three hundred and sixty-fifth day.

CHAPTER 8

Creativity and Faith Formation

For a number of years I have been engaged in faith formation and have observed groups of learners at various levels. I have always been amazed at how often children have been reluctant to come, how teachers have struggled with discipline problems and subject matter, and how families have found little excitement or creativity in religious education programs. This doesn't mean that the programs or catechists are not well prepared. Rather, the sessions often are marked by little innovation or creativity. Frequently, teachers and catechists are convinced that they must cover a particular amount of material. Faith itself is overlooked in an effort to make sure that the rules, traditional prayers, and the other "stuff" of religion are covered.

The Montessori Method

The content of the articles of our religion is important, but many catechists and teachers often neglect the total growth of the child (or of adults). Montessori principles, I found, include and develop the important area of faith so that the total person in all of his or her creativity can be nurtured.

Maria Montessori, an Italian physician and teacher, believed that no human person is educated by another. She believed that the teacher or facilitator was present to cultivate the individual's own natural desire to learn. In applying the Montessori theory to religious education, the facilitator would be allowing the faith of the learner to grow according to the Spirit's work in his or her life.

When I first delved into Montessori, a long-time facilitator reminded me that what I saw—the equipment of the classroom—was just a small part of the principles of good Montessori education. "Remember all of the principles," she said. "You won't go wrong, even if you have very little equipment to work with."

So, before setting up the room and deciding what to do, think about what is important in teaching religion. The first and guiding principle is that religion is a subject whereas faith is a way of life. When we try to teach one without the other, we fail. The difficulty is to include both because, although learners might be at the same level in the religious truths they have learned, they may not be at the same level in living the faith. Our programs need to allow for those different levels of faith and for the levels to be expressed in unique ways as only individuals made by a loving God can.

The use of the Montessori method in religious education allows for the combination of religious truths and living faith. With this loving approach, learners of any age might absorb and express their faith in their own way, allowing for "ah ha" moments and times of doubt. The classes are geared for those who are intent on rules as well as those who are ready for symbols, abstract beliefs, and mystery. The components of Montessori can be applied to almost every situation, allowing the creativity of the group to emerge.

Freedom

The first component of the Montessori approach is freedom. Freedom is defined as the ability to move about the meeting space without restraint. Maria Montessori believed that freedom was most important for learning because the learners were able to move from activity to activity according to their interests and needs, and at their own speed. She spoke of a "room in which all the children move about usefully, intelligently, and voluntarily without committing any rough or rude act."

This does not mean a lack of rules, but rather the opportunity for each learner to pursue interest at their own level of faith and religious knowledge. For example, two learners from separate families and backgrounds do not necessarily share the same interests. One might be interested in the story of Noah because that is the only bedtime story his mother ever told him. The other might be interested in the sacrament of baptism because his little sister will be baptized soon. In the Montessori classroom, each can pursue their interests. One learner seated in one area of the classroom can hear or read or act out the story of Noah, tell the story in his own words or work out puzzles about the story. The other learner can follow the ritual of baptism in another area, make a journal about his own baptism, and explore the symbol of water.

With this freedom both learners can study and internalize when they are ready, allowing for the action of the Spirit. Because of the principle of freedom, the meeting space is conducive to the expression of different faith levels. Learners are free to move about at will and free to choose their own activities.

Structure and Order

The second component is structure and order. This component allows for purposeful activity and calls for the meeting space to reflect the structure and order of the universe as

God made it. In the Montessori approach, the learner comes to trust the environment and his or her power to interact with it in a positive way. Learners are assured of a complete cycle, and since the materials have all the necessary pieces, there is no interruption when they are doing an activity and the materials are returned to the same place each time.

During their time in faith formation the learners decide what activities they wish to do. All the learners are able to begin right away because the materials are right there. They are able to carry their tasks to completion and learn to trust the universe around them.

Structure and order are important not only to our life on earth but also to our faith life. Faith exudes ritual and order. Structure and order are part of our worship, of our ritual and movement. God's presence in the universe is the model of order. The structure and order in the meeting space move the learner to realize that sense of rhythm, the power of the presence of God. Without this realization, faith is not possible.

Reality and Nature

The third component of the Montessori approach is reality and nature. This component is very down to earth, literally. It teaches the learners the limits of nature and reality. For example, learners find no duplicates of any activity, no matter how popular, and so appreciate the importance of taking turns. The reality of the world involves taking turns and helping one another; this is an important idea to learn. This component also allows for many hands-on experiences that can cause the learners to appreciate God's creation. The true Montessori room teems with creatures of all sorts and sizes. The children are able to observe and marvel and rejoice in God's creation as well as deal with the reality of death.

Shortly after beginning the Montessori approach, the reality and nature component is very much alive. Not only can you see it in taking turns but also in the regular good-bye rituals that take place for dead bugs and plants and in the memorials for grandmas and grandpas, friends and family who have died. Young learners better understand the rhythm of life through these simple actions.

Beauty

The fourth element in the Montessori approach is that of beauty and an atmosphere that encourages a positive response to life. Beauty is based on simplicity but also good quality design. This component invites participation and expresses a very powerful attribute of God.

In the Montessori session, the decorations, the equipment, everything reaches out and invites engagement. Bright colors, flowers, sounds, and pictures bring it to life. The atmosphere creates an appreciation of beauty in each other, a principle that Maria Montessori felt is so essential to the total growth of the learner.

Does the meeting space really have to look good? This could be difficult when the meeting space has to be set up each time because of space limitations. Do we have to work with beautiful materials? If our resources are limited, the beauty will come not from fancy equipment, nor from an attractive meeting space. It will spring from something else.

Beauty may manifest itself in the children. Each week a different learner is chosen and the group talks about what beauty is seen in them. We can note outward and inward beauty. We may talk about their special gifts from God.

Another special beauty of the week may be the prayer center. Needless to say, we may have some very unusual prayer centers, but one thing that never changes is their beauty, which is expressed by the children. God, indeed, is among us.

Montessori Equipment

The equipment or learning tools linked to the Montessori approach is the fifth component. Usually this component is what most people associate with the approach because it is the most visible. The equipment is to assist the learner's self-development by providing stimuli for concentration. The learning tools used in the regular Montessori classroom consist of a variety of items—the pink tower, the smelling jars, the sound boxes, the constructive triangles and more—that give learners the opportunities to explore.

When we do not have the actual Montessori faith equipment, we can start from scratch. If we are able, we can talk with Montessori teachers. We brainstorm how the regular Montessori equipment might be adapted to faith formation sessions. The timelines and the smelling objects can be adapted. Thinking creatively, any of the equipment in a regular Montessori classroom can be applied in some way to our faith. Timelines may center on different events in Scripture. Smelling objects are little canisters filled with the items to smell, including herbs and spices from the Holy Land.

In addition, we can create our own equipment. These might include blocks for building a church, puppets for Bible stories, activities that show God's presence around the world, candle painting that allows for the development of symbols, journal books, alleluia sticks in celebration of the resurrection, and more. Once we start on the equipment, we find that, although we wanted the fancy ready-made stuff, our creativity inspired by God can give us many more activities than we could imagine.

Development of Community Life

The final component of the Montessori approach is the development of community life. In this component learners develop a sense of ownership and responsibility. They become sensitive to each other and tolerant of those who are learning things they already know. Because they see the meeting space as belonging to them, they take care not only of the room but of each other.

I saw this component emerge in various ways in the learners I taught. One little boy became a natural leader. When we began a song about God, he would easily draw the others into the singing. Another girl was quick to point out and include each of the other family members in our prayer time. Still another child appreciated one-on-one contact with different people in the room.

I had the privilege of seeing one preschool group come alive because of the Montessori components. The children helped me understand more clearly how God can work through us if we recognize our ability to create alongside God. Many of the materials and ideas were not our own, but clearly came from the Spirit who inspired them. The idea of the "beauty" of the week, the prayer blanket for use during meditation, and the alleluia sticks were all the work of God creating through us. And all those creative encounters opened the door to yet other approaches.

Multiple Intelligences

In the early 1980s, Dr. Howard Gardner of Harvard University developed an educational theory that humans have not only several measurable intelligences but also one through which they learn best. Significantly he also stated that individuals are still capable of developing each of the intelligences.

The intelligences include verbal-linguistic (those individuals very good with words), logical-mathematical (those with strong math and logic tendencies), musical (those who possess an awareness of rhythm and music), bodily kinesthetic (those with physical talents), visual spatial (those able to convert ideas to concrete symbols), naturalist (those very attuned to classification), interpersonal (those who relate well to other people), intrapersonal (those with a strong understanding of themselves), and existential (those who grapple with the big questions of life).

The theory was and continues to be intriguing for me. It forces me to let my creative spirit come alive and causes me to move that kaleidoscope. It is not always easy but it is ever rewarding.

My first experience of actually using the multiple intelligences in a faith formation setting occurred with a group of educators during a week-long training at a local university. The first day, the session began with a Bill Peet story. Bill Peet, a children's author, often uses animals and their challenges to bring home lessons. The story I chose was about Chester, the Worldly Pig.

Chester did not want to be a pig. He wanted to be anything but. He tried his hand at the circus, as a baby, as a railroad worker, but nothing seemed to be his real vocation. He had just about given up when he discovered by accident that he had the map of the world in his skin markings. He had the gift, the vocation with him all the time. He just had to discover it.

During our time together I invited the catechetical leaders to discover their talent. What were they good at? What was the gift they could share that no one else could?

Then we launched into a creative drill that required them to think outside the box. I held up a scarf and a pencil. They were to think of things a scarf could be used for. They did the same type of exercise with a pencil. Finally I asked them to connect the scarf and the pencil, and to connect the ideas they came up with to something about God. Their minds were off and running. When we got to the intelligences, they were ready. Throughout the week we did all sort of exercises—some that worked and some that didn't. We saw what it meant to apply the intelligences to faith formation. We experienced first hand how our concept of God opened up when we danced and sang and classified and drew and talked and meditated and struggled.

Multiple intelligences and the Montessori components can become part and parcel of what we do. We have to be careful to always employ them with a beginner's mind so that we will be original in our work with the Spirit.

Our creativity flows from our body, mind, and spirit and we need to nurture all three if we are to grow in our faith. These two approaches to learning are able to make that happen while keeping us on our toes as we create with our Heavenly Father.

Something to Think About

- Where have I experienced freedom in my role as a religious educator?
- What does it mean to be part of a community?
- How do I nurture beauty in my faith life?
- What is my greatest fear in following the Spirit?
- Which of the intelligences am I strongest?
- What excites me about approaching faith formation in this way?
- How might I use the Montessori principles in my own work?

CHAPTER 9

Creativity and Intergenerational Learning

The group was a mixture of children, youth, and adults. They were gathered together to learn about the first part of the Apostles Creed. While they were waiting for everyone to arrive, I encouraged the participants to look around the room for signs of creation. We talked about their discoveries as the session began. "What does it mean to believe?" I asked. No one answered, so I pulled out a chair. "What do you believe about this chair?" I received the usual answers: It is brown. It is a chair. It was made by someone. When I asked if they believed the chair would hold them, they paused before they agreed that, yes, indeed, the chair would hold a person. Each of us puts this "belief" into practice every day.

We believe in God. What does this first line of the creed mean? By asking questions we held a discussion about who this God is whom we believe in. One eight-year-old girl said she believed in a God who really cared about whether or not she did her homework. Another child said he believed God was watching to see if he did anything wrong. More children chimed in, but not one adult shared in the discussion.

We then worked in small groups. Each was to draw a picture or make up a song or in some creative way show what his or her picture of God was. Again only the children's images of God emerged.

This continued through the presentation, regardless of the questions we asked or the activities we engaged in. The adults were there in body but not in spirit.

After the session was over, the adults complained that they had hoped to hear some solid explanations. They wanted to obtain new information about the first part of the creed, some information about its history and its place in our church. They said they were happy to be with their children but they didn't learn anything.

Was that true? I went home that night and thought about the session. The eight-year-old girl had spoken of a very personal God. The boy saw God just sitting there waiting for him to do something wrong. The drawings and presentations that the children and youth did contained shades of God and messages that shook and strengthened my faith. The adults may not have learned about history or a theoretical explanation of the creed. Instead, we had focused on the most basic aspect of the creed—belief. What is it I believe? What is it you believe? Unfortunately, the adults had not moved the kaleidoscope to look at the session in a new and different way.

A Fresh Outlook

Infusing creativity into sessions with mixed age groups means cultivating a beginner's mind, as well as a sharing of wisdom among persons on the various levels of the spectrum of faith growth. We enter the sessions with a new and fresh outlook, eager to find new ideas, original thoughts, inventive ways of looking at our faith. We look at what children say as a way to know God. Too often we adults feel that children have little to say about God, that children are just learning.

Children, however, often give us glimpses of God that adults overlook. God's creation is full of wonder; suffering is necessary for growth in people and animals; God gives us constant, unconditional love. All these glimpses of God may come from children, but we miss them if we think we've already heard what they have to say.

One grandmother in Minnesota used to say that we could learn a lot about God from children. After all, she reasoned, children were nearer to their time with God than she was at the ripe age of eighty-seven. Children were unspoiled, open, and direct. Not like us, she would muse, as we move further away from the day of our creation.

Her words contain a lot of wisdom. That grandmother realized that all the different occurrences in life, all the people along our paths have the opportunity to help us grow or keep us from growing, but that children are perhaps the most open of all when it comes to knowing about God.

Sharing Wisdom and Growing at Any Age

Once we approach mixed age encounters with a beginner's mind, both children and adults can share their wisdom with one another. What does it mean to grow in faith? What is most difficult? What is a joy? The outlook of a grandmother and the outlook of a nine year old are different, but the wisdom of each is worth listening to, reflecting on, and drawing inspiration from. If children see that we are open to learning from them, they will be more open to learning from us.

My daughter who lives and works in Washington, D.C., called one night, very excited about a discovery. She told me about meeting an older gentleman at a work gathering. She spent part of the evening talking with him about fund raising and politics and people. He was in his late sixties and my daughter Petra is twenty-two, an age when young people tend to think they know all there is to know. "Mom," she said, "he was so full of information, so full of insight. He spoke about many of the things we were talking about the other day, but somehow I could understand them more clearly coming from him. I guess I was ready to accept his wisdom."

How often are we ready to accept the wisdom of those older or younger than us? When we are receptive to what we can learn from others, regardless of their age, we become aware of yet another dimension of God—the ever-changing, ever-surprising, ever-insightful Supreme Being, manifest in the individuals around us.

Intergenerational Learning

Today parish programs are beginning to address learning as a whole community. Programs like the now-popular Generations of Faith aim to assist the parishes in educating the total community. Whole community catechesis is the rage. As good as this approach is, it is in danger of following many other approaches which, like shooting stars, burn brightly and then fizzle and die. The reason? Because although we talk about intergenerational learning, although we put together programs of intergenerational learning, often enough we don't *do* intergenerational learning. We often set aside our creativity and fall back on what has worked in the past, tweak it a little, and label it intergenerational learning.

Yes, we do bring together the different age groups. We prepare an opening and a closing section of the sessions when we gather the different ages together, but we may not always learn or celebrate together. In these meetings we like to believe that the approach we take is intergenerational learning, but this is true *only* if learning takes place *among* the generations.

For example, recently one evening an intergenerational learning session was planned at one of the local parishes. Before the session everyone shared a meal together. During the meal the adults were talking with one another and the children were sitting alone or running around. After dinner the program began with a prayer service composed of a reading, a song, and a brief reflection about the universe. Most of the children weren't interested because the speakers hadn't done anything to capture their attention. Even several of the adults held whispered conversations off and on throughout the service. When the service drew to a close, the groups were divided—parents and children going to one place, the youth to another, and individual adults to another. When the group time drew to a close, all the participants came together and shared what they had done in their groups. The adults seemed to merely tolerate the comments of the children. Everyone headed home, the intergenerational learning experience over.

Perhaps the experience would have been enriched if something was included in the meal to allow for interaction among the different age groups. The initial prayer service might have been more inclusive of all age groups. Why were the groups separated for the "learning" part? Instead of closing with a reiteration of what people learned, the session might have concluded with an element that challenged each participant to share their wisdom and listen to the wisdom of another.

Sometimes we hesitate to try new approaches because as a community we like to remain safe. We are often afraid of risk, of the unknown, and of failure. To go in a new direction, to be radically different is to allow the Spirit to work, instead of us. As long as we seek to control what we do, we will hamper the workings of creativity and the Spirit. This happens frequently when it comes to ongoing intergenerational learning.

New Approaches

The whole community can grow together but only if everyone—especially those responsible for faith formation—turn the kaleidoscope and approach one another with a fresh attitude. If a general session involves being spectators rather than participants, and separating into groups according to age level, that is not whole catechesis. That is what my grandmother would call "throwing a bone." The participants are together but not really. The bone is there but the meat is missing.

We need to allow our communities time to learn together totally. During a session not only should parents go with their children, but grandmothers and youth and single people and priests as well. Everyone in the community should look at a subject together and share their insights and growing wisdom so that all may deepen their faith. Opportunities can be provided for individual growth—prayer, sessions on the Bible, or history—according to interest and need. However, our parishes and our programs need to give more time for the total community to work, learn, laugh, and love together.

In one parish in Minnesota, confirmation was celebrated in the eleventh grade. As the faith formation team grew in their understanding of the sacrament and placed more trust in the Spirit, they moved to whole community catechesis for confirmation preparation. They recruited adults of all ages and backgrounds. During the sessions, each of the small groups was composed of youth and adults, some of whom were in their seventies. The whole community was told about the upcoming confirmation early on in the preparation. A banner was hung in the sanctuary with the names of all those seeking to celebrate confirmation, and parishioners were urged to "adopt" someone. Adoption meant praying for, and, if possible, meeting the individuals, talking with them, and getting to know them. Before confirmation, each candidate met individually with another adult in the parish to talk about what they had learned, to share their faith, and to become acquainted with each other. The confirmation ceremony and the various symbols were taught to the whole congregation and everyone, even the youngest children, helped prepare the reception following the celebration of the sacrament.

Confirmation preparation offers one opportunity for whole community catechesis. Although the experience wasn't perfect, each of the generations interacted, each shared its wisdom, often on a one-on-one basis. Everyone took part in this sacramental milestone in the teenagers' lives. Everyone knew the sacrament of confirmation was being celebrated, what was involved in the preparation, and why it was important. The whole parish helped many older people get in touch once again with what this sacrament meant.

Everyone Learning Together

When we plan for a community of believers of various ages to gather together to learn or to celebrate, we must be mindful to engage our creativity. Encourage both children and adults to use their beginner's mind. Everyone should be encouraged to drop any glimmer of sophistication so that we can all become as little children and really hear what God has to say to us. Programs can be offered that stimulate all of the intelligences and have all of the Montessori components so that people can experience the fullness of creativity and therefore the fullness of God.

Something to Think About

- What have I learned from someone older than me?
- What have I learned from someone younger than me?
- How do I envision people of different ages learning together?
- How do I imagine different ages being creative with one another?
- What can I do to become like a little child?
- What aspect of God was taught to me by someone not my age?

CHAPTER 10

The "Yes" That Echoes
through History

Mary was tired. She had just finished her morning chores and was going to settle down for a little time in quiet, listening to the sounds of the world around her, remembering the Lord and everything this good God had done for the people of Israel. She closed her eyes and listened to her breath go in and out, the rhythm of life, slowly in and out, much like the quiet flow of the day, an even pace, the steps on a journey.

Suddenly she heard something rustle. At first she thought it was that small, wild beast that had been seen in the streets, hungry and hurt, looking for food wherever it could find some. The thought of the leftover pita from last evening's meal came to her. Surely the animal would appreciate that. She rose to get it, but as she did, she staggered back. Her eyes shut automatically. A brilliant light, so bright that she could not open her eyes again, flooded the room. She could still see it through her closed lids, a light so strong she felt it light the recesses of her mind. What was happening? What was this strange light? Then she heard a sound.

The Message

"Mary, do not be afraid." The voice was gentle, lilting in quality, strong yet vulnerable. She felt her pulse slow, her heart slowly resuming its quiet beat. Her eyelids fluttered open. The light was still brilliant, but she could take it in without squinting. The figure in the light smiled at her. "Peace be with you, Mary. The Lord is with you and has greatly blessed you."

She bowed her head slightly. What do you say to a vision so full of life?

"Don't be afraid." Again the visitor repeated those words, and with the repetition, peace flooded through her.

"Why are you here?" she managed to murmur.

"You have found great favor with God. God has chosen you to be the mother of his son."

Mary let out an involuntary gasp.

"You will become pregnant and will bear a son who will be named Jesus. He will be great and will be called the Son of the Most High God. The Lord God will make him a king, and he will rule over the descendants of Jacob forever. His kingdom will know no end." The visitor, an angel of God, folded his outstretched arms back to his body. There was that dazzling smile again. "Your answer?"

Uncertainty welled up in her. "How can this happen? I am a virgin. I have never known a man."

The angel smiled. "Nothing is impossible with God. The Holy Spirit will come upon you, and God's power will rest on you. No man will be a part of this. This is why Jesus will be called the Son of God."

Mary tried to take it all in. Me? The chosen mother of the Savior? The mother of God? So many thoughts raced through her mind. What would this mean for her and Joseph? Who would believe her? What would people say about her pregnancy, especially her family? What would Joseph say? Her heart skipped a beat at that last thought. She loved Joseph and was looking forward to life with him.

They had just started to gather the things they needed for their new household. How would she convince him that she had not been unfaithful?

The angel added, "Mary, there's more. You might need this knowledge to make a decision." He waited for her to look up. "Your cousin Elizabeth is also with child, even though many have said she is too old to have children." He laughed. "I told you nothing is impossible with God."

"Really? Elizabeth with child?" Mary smiled broadly. She forgot all else. "I must go to her and see if I can be of help." She rose and began to talk to herself, listing all the things she needed to take with her.

"Mary." The angel tried to interrupt Mary's musings. Once he had her attention, he looked deep into her eyes, his light growing brighter as he did so. "I need an answer. Will you do what God asks of you?"

Mary paused to reflect. Would she do what God asked of her? Would she say yes to the God who had given her life itself? She saw all the difficulties before her as clearly as if they were happening now. She saw all the happiness. She knew what her answer would be.

I Am the Lord's Servant

"I am the Lord's servant. I am ready to do as God asks."

The angel let out a big sigh of relief. "Good. Then I will be on my way." He turned to leave, then turned back to face the young girl. "And thank you. For all of us." He smiled again, and before Mary could reply, he was gone.

Mary started to shake. What had she said yes to? Yes to being the mother of God? Such an enormous responsibility. I am the Lord's servant. I am the Lord's servant. Everything will work out. I trust in the Lord. She kept repeating those words in an effort to calm herself.

"Yes. Yes." The words came to her lips more easily each time. "I am the Lord's servant. I love my Lord." And with those words, the room was bathed in light once more.

This light was different. This light was soft and inviting, wrapping itself around Mary. She felt its gentle warmth and gradually relaxed. "I trust in the Lord," she murmured. "I love my God." The warmth enclosed her like a tight fitting robe, like a great hug.

As the sense of peace grew, she felt as if her heart would break in two because of the love she felt at that moment for her God. She didn't want it to end. She seemed to cross over into a world of ecstasy, a world in which she didn't have to think, she didn't have to worry. She only had to place herself in the hands of her Love and allow that Love to take her. She knew it was right. It was good. It was yes.

The light faded as quickly as it had come, but Mary knew that something was different. She was with child.

Mary Visits Elizabeth

Mary's parents hadn't understood the urgency of her visit to Elizabeth. Neither had Joseph. Mary's heart ached because she could not share with Joseph what had happened, but she felt she had to wait for the right time. Her meeting with Elizabeth was uppermost in her thoughts. Elizabeth was carrying the child who would proclaim the coming of the Savior. She wanted Elizabeth's advice about what to do.

Mary saw the roof of Elizabeth's home as she trudged up the hill. The morning sickness had delayed her start, and now the noon sun caused beads of sweat to form on her lips. She was almost there. One foot in front of the other. She would be all right.

"Mary!" Mary looked up to see Elizabeth standing at the top of the hill, her silhouette showing the growing child in her womb. Mary felt tears come to her eyes. Quickening her pace she met Elizabeth who made her way down the hill toward her.

"Elizabeth! I am so happy for you!" Mary caught her cousin in a warm embrace.

Elizabeth pulled away and looked at Mary. A smile lit her own face. "How is it that the mother of my Lord should come to me?"

"The Lord has done wonderful things, Elizabeth. I can hardly express my joy." Suddenly Mary stopped.

"Morning sickness." she grimaced. "I was hoping you could help me learn how to handle it."

Elizabeth laughed. "I am well past that, as you can see. But I do have some tips that I have learned." Elizabeth jolted upright and clutched her belly.

Concern enveloped Mary. "Are you all right? Should I get someone?"

Elizabeth looked down at her belly. "I think the baby is excited to meet his Lord also! He just did a summersault inside me!"

Mary grinned and pointed at her belly. "The only thing this little one is doing is pounding on my stomach to try and make room to grow."

Elizabeth put her arm around Mary. "Come, I have some herbs that will make the sickness better. And this discomfort will disappear as soon as the baby gets a bit bigger."

The two women walked up the hill together, one young and the other old. Both looked to each other for wisdom and support. Both sang the praises of a God who had done great things to them.

And as Mary and Elizabeth settled into sharing stories of God's work in their lives and tips on weathering the pregnancies, they grew tired. As they retired they knew that God was indeed good. And there was evening and morning on the three hundred and fifty-thousandth day of creation.

CHAPTER 11

Creativity in the Spiritual Life

We are able to see the sacred in every moment when we make creativity a part of our relationship with God and others. Yet, bringing creativity into our prayer life is often the hardest thing to do.

Many of us are used to having a very compartmentalized relationship with God. We pray at certain times. We pray using other people's prayers. We ask for things we need or help for people we care about. We read about meditation and centering prayer, trying each of them. When prayer doesn't seem to work for us, we feel we have failed, that we have missed something we are "supposed to do."

Remember when we were talking about the importance of play? Young learners find it easy to play because they don't have all the "supposed tos" in their life. This same factor applies to prayer. Some people pray and pray well because they don't have the "supposed tos" attached to their prayer life.

Not everyone is supposed to like centering prayer. Not everyone is supposed to like meditation. On the other hand, persons may like to use centering prayer, and others may be attracted to meditation provided they approach both practices in their own unique way. One person's form of meditation might be to sit quietly in a room and think about an aspect of God. Another person's meditation might be to walk through an arboretum and reflect on nature. Still another's meditation might consist in dancing, while reflecting on the creative marvel of the human body.

Creativity in our prayer and spiritual life enables us to develop our relationship with God in a very personal way. We acknowledge God's act of creation when God made us, and we respond accordingly in our own individual, creative ways.

Prayer is a way of life. There is no set time when we say, "This is prayer" and "This is not." All time is prayer if we approach it with that mindset. We are then able to remember that God is right with us all the time, helping us create, helping us deal with the difficulties that come our way, loving us into completeness every minute of every day.

Our prayer life needs that fullness if we are serious about growing in our understanding of sharing in creation. We need to incorporate that life-force into our prayer life so we can come to know our Creator better and so be more open to creative acts. It is the eternal circle of life.

Ordinariness of Prayer

Prayer is as simple as breathing in and breathing out, yet as difficult as becoming aware of our breathing. Because it is a way of life, prayer permeates everything we do. When we get up each morning, prayer is there. As we sleep, prayer is there. When we cook dinner, prayer is there. Prayer—our relationship with God—is everywhere. However, we have to become aware of it, much as we become aware of our breathing. We come to appreciate the wonder of it and take comfort in the fact that it is with us always, even when we don't recognize it.

When we pray as part of a routine or try to imitate someone else's prayer, we do not appreciate our own relationship with God. Picture yourself going up to someone and saying, "Would you mind breathing for me a while? I don't know how to do it on my own." Or worse yet, what if we get into the routine of breathing, and we don't recognize when our breath is raspy or that we are short of breath. A similar thing can happen with prayer. When we repeatedly do what others are doing because we think that is the "right" way, we fail to notice that we have not developed our relationship with God. When we encounter some problems or setbacks, they may go unnoticed until our spiritual life suffers.

Prayer can be ordinary but it can't be routine. Once it becomes routine, that means we are not being creative, not being ourselves in prayer. However, when prayer is ordinary, a fresh outlook will help us recognize the ordinary in a new spirit. That new spirit, by allowing creativity in, makes the ordinary extraordinary.

Prayer Paths Through the Ages

Many holy men and women have found various ways to develop their relationship with God, each as unique as the person. Brother Lawrence of the Resurrection, a seventeenth century Carmelite, would stop during the ordinary activities of the day to become aware of God's love; he called it practicing the presence of God. Therese of Lisieux practiced her Little Way; she saw the opportunity to grow closer to God by making simple acts of sacrifice for her sisters in religion, as well as for others. Ignatius of Loyola initiated a series of spiritual exercises which were a means of great growth for him. He brought the Scriptures to life by imagining what the persons in the stories were thinking and feeling, delving into why they did the things they did.

These saints found means of relating to God that were attuned to who they were, to their uniqueness. We have to do likewise. Creativity in prayer is not something new. Different prayers emerge from the different faiths. Drumming and yoga, mantras and breathing, mindfulness and loving kindness, tai chi and Sufi dancing, the rosary and contemplative prayer are all ways in which people have expressed their uniqueness.

Using the Intelligences in Prayer

In order to get a "right fit" for our prayer, when we talk about approaching God with creativity, we may find it valuable to turn to the multiple intelligences and the Montessori components. These approaches can also assist us in responding to God in the way that best matches our personality. For persons whose strength is the bodily kinesthetic intelligence, meditative walking may be a good prayer. For the visual spatial individual, sketching from nature can be a good touch point with God. Persons of each type of intelligence can pray in their own unique way.

Verbal Linguistic Intelligence

For persons whose strength is verbal-linguistic intelligence, one of the best books to broaden their approach to prayer may be *Finding God in the Dark* by John Pungente and Monty Williams. The authors relate the spiritual exercises of St. Ignatius to certain movies. Through the fifty-two films in the book, a person is able to make watching the films in the Ignatian spirit an act of contemplative prayer and self-reflection. Other prayer possibilities might be using mantras or developing prayer collections.

One woman I know simply talks aloud to God while she works around the house. She has reached the point where she pauses during her conversation to listen. "Not only do I gain great insight while I'm talking and viewing things in a good context, but when I learned to pause and listen, I was blown away by what God had to say to me."

Logical Mathematical Intelligence

Persons who learn mainly through logical mathematical intelligence thrive on connections. Something as simple as a family photo can launch these persons into a deeper understanding of what it means to be in relationship with God. The examination of conscience is another very good prayer exercise for someone of this intelligence. Through a brief examination of the day's activities, connections for growth can be made, and their prayer time will be filled with opportunities for growth.

Sometimes I use the examination of conscience before I go to bed. I am aware that I constantly zero in on one or two aspects of my spiritual life. These are habits that have surfaced time and again. The examination challenges me to face why I haven't made any changes in these areas, and why I continue to allow them to fester in my life. This prayer is not complicated but it is effective in enabling me to make connections with my behavior.

Musical Intelligence

Persons blessed with musical intelligence will find writing or painting a song creative ways for communicating with God. Becoming aware of the rhythms of life will launch a musical person off into avenues of thought not common in other prayer forms. One example of using musical intelligence in prayer is the Chalice of Repose Project, which offers a loving presence to anyone who is dying. In teams of two or three, the members keep vigil at the person's bedside, playing music designed to meet the needs of the dying person. The music engages the whole person and affects their thinking and feeling. The musicians in prayer offer the dying a supportive community and an unconditional loving presence. What a beautiful expression of creative prayer!

Visual Spatial Intelligence

Using icons as a launch for prayer is a creative means for persons with visual spatial intelligence. Someone once told me that she looked on icons as a "Where's God?" tool much akin to the popular "Where's Waldo?" books. She said she looks at the icon and lets the images reveal God to her. God might be in the piercing eyes or the outstretched hands. God might peek out of a symbol in a column or the color of the clothing. She prays with the icon, open to God working in her, and comes away from her time of prayer with new insights into who God is in her life.

Other ways in which visual spatial persons have come to prayer have been through the use of sacred space and of symbols—traditional ones like the Stations of the Cross or self-created ones that remind them of new insights.

Bodily Kinesthetic Intelligence

These persons may pray as they dance, as they clap, and as they walk. They throw their whole body into prayer. Many bodily kinesthetic persons find that walking is a deeply meditative prayer form. Whether through an awareness of how they walk, completely immersing themselves in the walk itself, or through the focused thinking that yields insights about God, they are happy to use their whole selves for communication with their Maker.

Labyrinths, a good prayer form especially for persons of both the bodily kinesthetic and the existential intelligences, involve following a path that directs the walkers in only one direction, allowing them to move and focus, reflecting on a challenge, choice, or an event in their life. Sometimes we are unable to find a labyrinth, or we are not able to use our whole body. In this instance, the prayer can be done using only fingers on a paper labyrinth. A person is able to walk along the "path," concentrating on his or her motion, allowing his or her mind to become free so as to concentrate on God.

Naturalist Intelligence

This intelligence lends itself well to ritual, both in participation and creation. Anything in creation can become part of those rituals or a means for further contemplation with God. Clouds and bugs and plants all aid the person in focusing on God and developing an awareness of God's presence around us.

Artist Jennifer Steinkamp has created a life-sized tree using digital photography and movement. The "Tree" was on display recently at the Kemper Museum of Modern Art in Kansas City. The tree goes through the seasons, moving and bending, the trunk firmly rooted. Yet it is able to change from new leaves to fruit to color to bare branches. What a meditative time! To draw the cycles of life, the spirit of God on the earth from such a simple thing is the hallmark of the naturalist intelligence.

Interpersonal Intelligence

Persons whose strength is this intelligence thrive on community prayer, especially the Mass. When the liturgy is done well, these people leave refreshed and renewed. God has touched them in a most unique way.

I have had the privilege of participating in prayer services, sometimes in my clown persona. A dear clown who is always doing something wrong is present with the community to show them that despite the times we turn from God, God is still there, loving us and welcoming us back to community. Interpersonal people relate well to this prayer which helps them see the universal traits shared by all humankind.

Intrapersonal Intelligence

Journaling is one of the finest forms of prayer for the intrapersonal "pray-er." Through journaling, such persons are able to delve into what their strengths and weaknesses are and perceive how to use these insights to grow in faith.

The practice of mindfulness, while helpful for every person, is especially so for those with strong intrapersonal intelligence. Mindfulness is a state of awareness in which you pay close attention to the present moment. You may practice it throughout the day. Persons with intrapersonal intelligence are able to make connections between God and their day-to-day activities.

Existential Intelligence

This is the intelligence of those who grapple with the big questions of life. For these individuals, using a wanted poster can move the individual closer to God and the community. We are challenged to come to an understanding of why the wanted person would commit such a crime and how we can find it in our hearts to forgive him or her. Sometimes we find forgiveness is indeed a difficult task.

Solitude is a part of life. We need it in order to grow, just as the farmer needs to let the land lie fallow for a time if he or she wants the seeds to be planted later to grow well. In the prayer of solitude, the individual becomes aware of the presence of God, then proceeds to empty himself or herself of all thoughts and feelings, letting God and only God be present.

Working through any of the intelligences is sure to draw you closer to God, developing a deeper and more exciting friendship. For further prayer experiences using the intelligences, read the book, *Prayer and Multiple Intelligences: Who I Am Is How I Pray* (Twenty-Third Publications).

Finding God in the Components

Creativity in spirituality can reach its apex through the use of the Montessori components.

With *freedom* in our spiritual life, we are able to view anything as a source of growth for our friendship with God. We will respect, not only for ourselves but for others, the freedom to seek God at our own level of faith and religious knowledge. Our acceptance of one another will deepen our understanding of each other as brothers and sisters.

Structure and order enable us to enjoy a friendship with God within the eternal circle of Life. We will see more clearly the purpose of our lives and how that fits into the universe. The importance of daily interaction with God and others is an important part of building God's kingdom on earth.

Closely related to structure and order are *reality and nature*, which teach us how limited we are without the community. We realize how we can accomplish so much more through interaction with others than if we work alone.

Beauty challenges us to discover God within everyone and everything, while the Montessori equipment, the multiple intelligences, or other means we use to enrich our prayer life offer us many opportunities to nurture that beauty.

Finally, the *development of community* will become a longing in our lives if we open ourselves to growth. We will actively seek times when we can draw nourishment and insight from others making the journey, as well as be open to what we can learn about God from them.

Of course, the greatest source of creativity in the spiritual life is God. By being open to God working in us, we can see and feel and taste the Divine in the little moments. Through the multiple intelligences and the Montessori components we trust God to work with us.

We will be with God as we wash the dishes. We will taste God in the kiss of our loved ones. We will see God in the neighbor sharing a tool. We will hear God in the silence of reflection. We will smell God in cooking supper. Most importantly, we will come to know God creatively in each other and ourselves. We will know the truth of what is written in Isaiah 65:18: *"Be glad and rejoice forever in what I am creating."*

Something to Think About

- How do I define prayer?
- What has been my experience of praying in different ways?
- What "shoulds" have I placed on my prayer life?
- When have I felt God in my prayer?
- How can I apply the Montessori components in my spiritual life?
- Based on what I have read, how will prayer transform the world?
- Do you think God prays?

CHAPTER 12

Creativity in Community

One of my warmest memories is tied to a family "ritual" that took place at 4:30 each afternoon. This was shortly before my father returned home from work. My mother, brothers, and sisters would begin preparing for supper. One of us set the table. Another opened the canned fruit for dessert. Yet another poured the drinks. My mother was at the stove, putting the finishing touches to the meal.

Once my father walked through the front door, the ritual began: a kiss for my mother, hellos to the kids, a walk to the closet to hang up his coat, and then the move into the kitchen to his chair at the head of the table. We all followed suit, taking our respective chairs, jumping up only to get the salt or in answer to a request from my mother. We said grace, and then the heart of the meal began.

My sister Florence would regale us with stories of her after-school work in the neighborhood bakery, telling us how cream puffs were made or how many brownies were sold in one hour. My brother Paul would complain about something at his after-school job or talk about his shop class. My brother Casey would ask questions about a story in the evening paper. I would generally take it all in or argue with anyone who was willing to take me on. My father would talk about his day at the railroad, and my mother would fill us in on happenings in the neighborhood or with the rest of the family. Even after the plates were empty and stomachs were full, we would sometimes sit around and talk. This was our community time.

The family table is one of the strongest expressions of community. It has the power for joining and strengthening those gathered around it. In *The Surprising Power of the Family Table*, Miriam Weinstein describes how the simple family table can teach reading, solve difficulties, and improve the quality of daily life. Perhaps because of all this and more, Jesus chose the family table as the center of our faith.

The Family Table of Faith

The family table of faith is the time we gather to worship, to remember the stories, to learn the lessons, to break the bread, and to create together. The act of worship enables us to grow with one another, to celebrate our life and creativity.

At the time of the early Christians, the family of faith gathered in individual homes or in secret, hiding from those who wanted the Christians dead. Those brave men and women of faith would gather by candle light, the old and the ill having the only available seats. The rest found space on the floor to sit or lie or kneel and several stood with arms folded or outstretched. Each chose a unique creative stance to bring to the table.

Without books, they sang from memory, sometimes composing a song on the spot. Others danced to the music, moving their bodies in praise before their Creator. When the songs were exhausted, the family moved to story-telling, remembering accounts of Jesus, of Moses and David, of Saul and Peter. They talked and shared these stories with expressions dancing across their faces, the vibrancy of their faith evident in their creative tales.

The time then came for the family to share their "ah ha" moments, the times when God had touched their lives, when Jesus had shown them the way. They talked of lessons learned and of the Spirit alive and at work in their lives. They laughed, they cried, and they hugged one another.

When it came time to share the bread, they first remembered those not present with them, those sick or in need, and those who had already entered the kingdom of heaven. All of the family were present at that moment of the breaking of the bread and the sharing of the cup. Those early Christians were able to see Christ in the bread and wine because they were able to see Christ in one another, through the songs and stories and "ah has" and prayers flowing with creative life. As the time at the family table came to a close, the head of the family urged them all to go out and love and serve the Lord and each other. The Christians did this by loving and serving through their unique gifts, allowing themselves to share in creative action with God, enabling them to reach the family of believers at all stages, whether the persons were firm in the faith, wavering, or had not yet discovered God. The early Christians knew what it meant to be a community, a family of believers.

Today we do not hide to worship, but some persons hide in their homes, afraid to gather for worship. Many have lost the creative life that once infused our communities. Some persons lobby for the right to own concealed weapons so they can protect themselves from intruders. Teachers, nurses, and other caregivers don't hug children because they might be accused of being sexual predators. Many of us are suspicious of anyone different from us.

Some of our neighborhoods have fallen to ruins or are silent as most of the people work long hours, returning home well after dark and when it's too late to play outside with the kids. Our faith, which once was shared at picnics and over backyard fences, is often silent.

Creativity Resurrected

People sometimes complain about how times have changed. They talk about the lost neighborhoods and bemoan the change in manners of children and youth. Reminiscing about home fires, they recall how the family was once a close-knit unit. After complaining and sharing memories, they leave but have no plans to change the situation.

When we accept our calling to be co-creators with God, we respond to the needs around us. We use our creativity, our very life, to move the creation around us toward good and toward growth. What exactly does that mean?

In the Pastoral Constitution on the Church in the Modern World one section reads, "To those, therefore, who believe in divine love, [God] gives assurance that the way of love lies open to all people and that the effort to establish a universal brother and sisterhood is not a hopeless one. He cautions them at the same time that this love is not something to be reserved for important matters, but must be pursued chiefly in the ordinary circumstances of life."

"[Love] must be pursued chiefly in the ordinary circumstances of life." Responding to this command means responding in love to family, to neighbors, to casual acquaintances, even to strangers with a divine love and care, the kind of love that transforms and is without fear.

Reformation

Once I heard a story about a woman who lived alone on the outskirts of a town. For days she had read reports about an escaped convict in the area, a convict who was presumed to be armed and dangerous. She wasn't afraid. She was used to stories of prisoners on the run—after all, she lived on one of the major highways that ran past the state prison. To her it was just a story on the radio.

One morning she went into her kitchen and found a man seated at her kitchen table, a pistol lying at his right hand. She smiled at him and began to make some tea.

"What kind of tea do you like?" she asked, filling the kettle.

"Lady, what are you doing? Sit down," he growled.

"Nonsense. We won't have any breakfast if I sit down." She plopped a cutting board and a knife and two huge red apples in front of him. "If you cut up the fruit, I'll scramble the eggs." She bustled about the kitchen, gathering the breakfast items. Then she cracked the eggs and got the bacon sizzling. The woman asked her "visitor" to cut some slices of bread when he was finished with the fruit. Soon the two of them were sitting in front of plates heaped high with breakfast vittles guaranteed to make anyone's mouth water.

The man reached for his fork and started to eat. She reached for his hand, looked him in the eye, and said, "We first thank the Lord who gave us this food."

In bewilderment he put down his fork and bowed his head.

She began, "Lord, we thank you for this food, for the hands that helped it grow and that gathered it. We thank you for the animals who gave their lives for us. We thank you for those who prepared it. We thank you that we can love you and each other. Amen."

Together the two of them feasted. As they did, they talked, and the stories came out of hurt, of distrust, of sadness, and of anger. They talked and talked into the afternoon. Two people sharing and respecting one another. As the afternoon drew to a close, the man agreed to return to the prison, his escort being the woman with whom he had shared breakfast. This was one woman who loved enough to meet that man as her brother.

How many of us would respond in a similar manner? Not many, and yet that is what God asks us to do—to pursue love in the ordinary circumstances of life. What is more ordinary than sharing breakfast with another person? What is more ordinary than gathering at the family table?

In order to pursue love in the ordinary circumstances of life, we need creativity. We need the beginner's mind that allows us to respond in ways that help us turn the kaleidoscope. We plan the neighborhood block party with our ears closed to the "it just doesn't work" chants from others. We work to draw the neighbors together in parties or dinners or play times, ignoring comments of "they just want to be by themselves."

We get to know our neighbors' names and their lives, the names of their children and what their children like. We involve ourselves in their lives as the brothers and sisters they are to us.

When we do that, we begin to resurrect our neighborhoods. We begin to infuse life and love into them. We become the power of change needed in the world, and suddenly things begin to happen. Faith sharing takes place, people share their things and their ideas. Individuals begin to care about each other. We shelve our suspicions and trust in God.

Creativity Meets Helplessness

People are often divided about what is happening to our world. Many blame the government for thinking only of profit and not people. Others blame the media, claiming that they play on the fears and suspicions of people. So many feel helpless.

Whatever the reason, we need to examine the overriding force that drives out life, drives out creativity. That force is fear. Whether through the government or the media, our next door neighbor or someone who looks different from us, fear keeps us from loving. We fail to trust that God will take care of us, no matter what. Fear breeds our helplessness.

When we bid goodbye to our fear, when we recognize the power of God, we are able to respond in creative ways. News reports of war signal us to nurture our peace-making abilities on a large scale: diplomacy, protests, negotiations, or on a small scale: teaching children how to resolve conflicts, loving an "enemy," learning about other cultures for the sake of understanding. Pictures of famine-ravaged countries move us to examine how we use food. We begin composting, or set aside the cost of a daily meal and earmark it for an organization working with famine relief. We stretch our limits and volunteer to work in other countries to literally feed the hungry.

Each media news event can cause us to re-evaluate how we respond in creative ways. With that response, we can love in ordinary but powerful ways. We look at the world through a beginner's mind, changing the curve of that kaleidoscope. With that fresh view we can make connections and birth new responses that keep us from nurturing fear and a sense of helplessness.

T.S. Elliot wrote, "When the stranger says, 'What is the meaning of this city? Do you huddle together because you love one another?' What will you answer? 'We all dwell together to make money from each other,' or 'This is community'?"

Through working and responding as sharers in creation, we can transform our families, our communities, and the world. Then we can pray with the words of Psalm 133:

"Behold, how good and how pleasant it is for people to dwell together in unity."

Something to Think About

- Growing up, what were my family meals like?
- What did I learn from them?
- When do I feel united with my faith community?
- What causes me to fear?
- What do I see as a problem in the world today?
- How can I respond creatively to this problem?
- What do I give to my community?
- How can my community be stronger? Name concrete ways.

Chapter 13

An Experience of Transformation

"I don't understand why he wouldn't let us build some tents." Peter wasn't watching where he was going, and he was scattering stones in every direction as he walked. "It wouldn't have cost too much."

"I don't think that was why he didn't want it," said James, trying to keep the falling pebbles from landing between his toes or caught between his sandals and his feet. "He wanted us to remember what happened and not be dependent on tents or other things to remind us. He wanted us to commit the experience to our memories."

John just held his tongue, quietly basking in the past moment. What had just occurred was something he still couldn't make sense of, and he wasn't sure if any of them understood. Jumping to avoid a stone loosened by Peter's angry feet, he decided it was time to say something.

"Hold on, just a minute." He pulled at the robes of both men. "Let's just sit down and talk a minute. Doing this as we head down this mountain is getting us nowhere." He looked at Peter directly. "And it isn't helping your temper one bit, Peter."

Peter scowled at John but dropped to the ground. He dug out his water flask and took a long drink. James sat down beside him and John was last, coming to rest at Peter's feet.

"What did we see up there, Peter?" John hoped that by talking, it would become clear to all of them.

Peter's scowl deepened. "You know darn well what happened up there."

"Tell me anyway. Let's see if we all saw the same thing."

James nodded in agreement. He took a cracker from his pocket and bit into it.

Recalling What Happened

Peter cleared his throat. "Okay. I'll humor you." He stared off into the distance. "The light is what I remember first. So brilliant. And then I noticed Jesus' gown. No one, but no one could get it as white as that gown was. I just had to close my eyes. It hurt to look at such brightness."

"Me, too," James chimed in. "I couldn't keep looking. And in a way, I still wanted to look, even if it hurt. It was like something I wanted but wasn't ready for."

"Did you two hear voices?" John looked from one to the other.

"Of course we heard voices!" Peter's own voice raised a couple of levels. "You heard voices. James heard voices. We all heard voices."

"So I wasn't imagining it," John said.

"For pity's sake, John, you saw them. As big as life. Moses and Elijah. You couldn't mistake them."

James scratched his head. "That's what I can't figure out. We've never seen Moses or Elijah. Never met them, only heard the stories. And yet we knew. We knew who they were without anyone telling us."

John nodded in agreement. "I felt the same way. I had never seen them, yet I knew. I knew them as surely as I would know my mother."

Peter laughed. "Do you think when Jesus called them by name, that's why we knew who they were?"

John made a face. "I don't remember hearing Jesus say anything."

"Me either," offered James.

"Well I did," Peter sputtered.

"Are you sure?" John looked directly into Peter's eyes.

Peter hesitated, twisting his robe between his fingers. "I can't be sure but I think I heard Jesus call them by name."

"But you're not certain?" John's eyebrow lifted in question.

Peter picked a wildflower that was tickling his leg. "All right. I can't be certain. I might not have heard their names." His face brightened. "But then again I can't be certain that I didn't hear their names."

James started to say something. John put out his hand and touched James' arm. "Let's just suppose it could have been either way. What happened next?"

Peter's face began to turn red. The blonde wisps of what was left of his hair stood on end. He cleared his throat.

John repeated his question. "What happened next?"

Peter drew in the sand. He swallowed. "I...I...I fell asleep."

James looked at Peter in astonishment. "I did too. I didn't want to admit it because I thought you would laugh."

John laughed. "Look at the three of us. All of us asleep and none of us willing to admit it."

The Voice of the Lord

"But what woke you up?" Peter brushed off a spider that was climbing on his sleeve. His anticipation of the answer was palpable.

"The voice." John squeezed his hands together. "The voice woke me."

Silence settled on the three men. Only the faint whisper of the wind as it brushed through the fig branches ruffled the quiet. Finally Peter spoke.

"This is my own dear Son with whom I am well pleased."

James and John joined in.

"Listen to him." The three voices spoke as one.

James paused and then squeaked. "The voice of Yahweh." Three heads bowed in unison, remembering.

John's chuckle broke into the quiet. "And all three of us huddled together like frightened children."

The other two men guffawed.

"It isn't every day that Yahweh is so direct in speaking to me," said Peter, wiping tears from his eyes.

"Nor to me," added James. "And right away I wondered if I had been listening to Jesus as well as I should." He paused, remembering. "Yahweh was pretty definitive about listening to his Son."

"Well, we listened when Jesus came to us. We were huddled together, and he told us not to be afraid." John stood up. "I don't know about you two, but almost immediately a tremendous sense of peace and well-being came over me. I wasn't afraid. I had heard the voice of God. I had seen Elijah and Moses. I had witnessed a real change in Jesus, yet I wasn't afraid."

Peter looked up at John. "The change you speak of was the transformation of our Master. We were privileged to witness his full glory. The glory that will come when he rises on the third day as he has told us." Peter stood to join John. "We have been privileged to see what is to come. We have been drawn into Yahweh's river of love and knowledge. We have seen a glimpse of the fullness of God, of the flow of creation."

John and James remained silent, taking all that Peter said into their hearts.

James took a deep breath and finally spoke. "I think that means that we too shall shine as brightly someday. Remember I told you it was something I felt destined for but wasn't ready for? It's that fullness, it's that flow." He shook his head. "Nothing could be better."

John smiled to himself. Not only had he been able to relive the experience, but he had diverted Peter's mind from the tents. He started on down the hill.

The Question of the Tents

"Hey, wait," Peter called. John stopped and looked back. "We still haven't talked about the tents. Why Jesus didn't want the tents. I said I would get three—one for him, one for Elijah, and one for Moses. People could come and pray and remember."

James was immediately caught up in the plan. "We could actually build them out of cedar so they wouldn't blow away in a strong wind. Plus the cedar would keep the odor of the offerings always before Yahweh."

"That's a good idea, James," Peter said, patting him on the back. "In fact we could make hangers on the wall for lanterns so that the cedar 'tents' would be lit all the time. The smell and the light before God always."

"And then…" James was interrupted by John.

"But remember, Jesus said no." John looked toward the top of the mountain. "He said, 'Don't tell anyone about what you have seen until the Son of Man has been raised from the dead.' I think that not telling others includes not building tents or little cedar houses."

Peter and James looked at each other. John was right. Jesus had specifically told them to say nothing to anyone.

A nervous chuckle escaped Peter's lips. "I guess tents or cedar houses would draw a bit of a crowd. And then people would ask questions, we would have to explain, and then...."

James jumped in. "And then the Pharisees would have even more reason to hate Jesus."

Peter nodded. "No tents. No cedar houses." He turned to John. "But how will we remember? We grow old. We forget. And I don't want to forget this. How will we remember?"

A Time to Remember

John puzzled over what Peter said. He didn't want to forget either. How would they remember? And then, as clear as could be, the answer came to him. He looked at his two friends and smiled.

"It's in the flow. We all felt it. At that moment we saw the fullness of creation, we felt the flow of the Spirit through us. That's how we'll remember. Whenever we are blessed enough to feel that as we preach the word of Jesus, when we shout Yahweh's praise, we will feel the moment of transfiguration. We won't need tents or memories or pictures. We'll have the experience again and again."

Peter puzzled over the words and then took John's hand. "You mean that whenever I share with people the love I feel for Jesus or tell them of the times I trust my Savior, the times I can love as he loves, I can feel the flow of that creation through me, as much as I did today?"

John nodded. "It won't be every time, but there will be special times. We'll know. And no one can take them from us because they will be a part of us, God in us, creating, transforming, growing."

Peter started down the hill. "This certainly beats tents. And who knows, maybe someday others will come to recognize it. They, too, will feel God in them, creating, transforming. They, too, will know the flow we feel today."

James ran after him. "But there will probably always be those who want to build tents."

John laughed out loud and hurried to catch up with his two good friends.

As John and James and Peter settled into bed that night, they each fell asleep aware of God transforming them, bringing them to the fullness of creation. And God said it was good, and there was evening and morning on the five hundred and seventy-four thousandth day of creation.

CHAPTER 14

The Journey to Wholeness

Who knows God? We know bits and pieces, and even those bits and pieces change as insights grow. To borrow from E.L. Doctorow and his insight on writing a novel, discovering God is like driving a car at night. You can only see as far as your headlights, but you can make the entire journey to God that way. Knowing God is a creative process.

When children are young, babes in arms, they come to know God in the arms of their mothers, rocking them to sleep or cuddling them as they eat. As they grow, they learn of God's love through their fathers and their aunts and uncles and other caring adults. They grow in their knowledge of God as they learn about their world—the many trees, the beautiful flowers, and the variety of animals. And so it continues throughout their lives.

There is no magic time in adulthood when the process stops, when we know God completely. We still know only bits and pieces. Despite this truth, some people feel they know everything about God. They speak definitively about God. God is as they say. There is no room for new knowledge. These people will confidently list what God is and what God isn't. It is as if they have had a private conversation with God, and during that time they learned all there is to know about God. How un-infinite that is!

As we journey—and each person's journey is unique—we discover different faces of God. If we use our creativity, we can come to discover the true infinity of God. Infinite is defined as having no boundaries or limits, immeasurably great or large, boundless. Our creativity, then, is able to imagine and to discover and to wonder at a God who has no limits.

Because God is infinite, we can change our idea of God almost daily. In grade school I saw God as someone ready to punish me if I did anything wrong. As I learned more about God, that image changed to a God who, yes, was concerned that I do right but who also loved me. In college, my kaleidoscope changed again, and I found a personal God who loved and cared about me very deeply. As I learned more about multiple intelligences, my image of God grew in yet another direction. I discovered a God who laughed and cried and danced and wondered. My kaleidoscope keeps changing and as it does, new discoveries about God are made.

When we don't box God in, when we allow our creative selves to discover God anew each day, we have a natural, creative, Spirit-filled growth in all of our relationships.

In addition, we are better able to be open to creating. We can cast aside the thoughts of failure or of what people will think. We can look with confidence to following in God's footsteps and making a new world with each step we take.

When I was in college, I worked at a day care center in the inner city. There, among two and three year olds, I learned about God. The day care wasn't a religious school, but, during times of play, times of reading, and nap time with no sleep on the horizon, insights of God surfaced. Those children taught me

- God loves us no matter what
- God is a mystery no detective can solve

- God is everything
- God is when I'm happy and when I'm laughing
- God knows everything, even more than Santa
- God is a puzzle
- God is everything great and small
- God connects us to everything and everyone
- God loves us even when we do bad things
- God holds me tight every day

That list never grows old. Each day it opens up new vistas of God for me. It allows me to share creation with God and be confident that God will see the creation through to its fullness. With the God whom those children described to me, no room is left for fear. This description of God only opens wider vistas that I can't even imagine. God gives this gift, this opportunity to each of us. When we say yes, we open the door to a delightful journey to wholeness.

Pope John XXIII responded to God much like the driver at night with his headlights. John XXIII's greatness, according to the Russian Orthodox theologian, Alexander Schmemann, was that he was not afraid to be open to ideas that could not be contained in neat parcels. He didn't have to see the end of the road in order to have the courage to take the first steps.

What we need to do is turn on our headlights and trust the Spirit to take us on the entire journey. Then we will be free to create along the way, receptive to the ideas of whomever we meet.

Something to Think About

- What has my journey in faith been like up to this point?
- How has my image of God changed since childhood?
- What is my image or vision of God today?
- What makes it difficult for me to trust in God?
- How do I travel on my journey? Do I need neat parcels or am I open to chaos?
- Of the children's images of God, which reveals an aspect of God for me?
- What keeps me from taking the first steps to being a co-creator?

CHAPTER 15

Sharing in God's Creation

Throughout this book we have seen that we are called to be co-creators with God. From the very first day after the creation of man and woman, God called us to walk beside him and create. Through this creation we come to know more and more about God. Through this creation we come to know ourselves and the God in us. We learn to live.

Unfortunately we lose our belief in this calling somewhere along our life's journey. We don't use our creativity. We worry about what people will think. We pass up something new because we think that the way we have always done things must be the right way. Getting the right answer becomes a priority in our lives. In addition, we worry about breaking rules, about crossing into new territory.

Sadly, we have forgotten how to play because of all the rules which say we must behave a certain way at a certain age. The saddest thing of all is that we have come to believe that we are not creative. Creativity, we say, is for a chosen few. "I am not creative" has become our battle cry.

Creativity is stifled in us in lots of different ways. We evaluate things before they have an opportunity to come to birth, or we compete with one another. Instead of letting learning flow, we tell ourselves and our children exactly how to do things. Activities are rationed or chosen for us, instead of letting us choose what is best at the time for our growth. We always put the pressure on to succeed, to be right, to be noticed. We rush, rush, rush, without enough time to do anything.

God doesn't want any of this. Rather, God would have us keep our time open-ended so we could work together or alone, letting creative idea after creative idea flow to completion. Our vocation is to bring to life the God hidden inside us. God is calling us to bring God forth into the world by using our creativity.

Chuck Jones, the animator who brought the infamous Wile E. Coyote to life, once said that in order to draw a coyote "you have to have a coyote inside of you and you have to get it out." Jones had to "give birth" to a coyote. God dwells in us, waiting to come out. We can bring the God in us "out" by making connections, by cultivating a beginner's mind, by always turning that kaleidoscope. Above all, we have to trust in the Spirit, give control to God, and always be a fool for Christ. Perhaps we need to heed the words of the poet Rumi.

> *Forget safety*
> *Live where you fear to live*
> *Destroy your reputation*
> *Be notorious.*
>
> *I have tried prudent planning*
> *Long enough, from now*
> *On, I'll live mad.*

Let's forget about living safely. Take the risk necessary for creative growth. We can stretch ourselves to new heights and involvement, and we can risk people talking about us. We have been staid for too long. We need to take the leaps that will bring us into the fullness of the kingdom of God.

May we all be mad for God, joining in the exciting journey of co-creation and weaving the web of the Spirit throughout the world.

Something to Think About

- How willing am I to risk being creative?
- What is stopping me from responding to God?
- Am I willing to take a creative leap of faith? Why or why not?
- What do I find helpful when it comes to creativity?
- How have I given birth to God in the world?
- What one thing am I going to do to nurture my creativity?
- In what area in my life can I say yes to God and yes to being a co-creator?
- What excites me about being creative?
- How can I support others in being co-creators?
- What is God saying to me now?

CHAPTER 16

Creativity around the World

The day dawns bright and sunny. In a small town in Kansas, a farmer greets the day while walking from the barn with a pail of fresh milk. As the sun rises, the golds and yellows of the wheat tickle the pinks of the morning sky.

Farther east in New York City, a skater takes to the ice in Central Park. Soon sleek, smooth marks trace across the ice. She jumps, vaulting high into the air in a motion of strength and beauty.

In a small village in Ireland, a shepherd herds his flock up an emerald hill. He watches as the sheep climb, forming what looks to be a chain of pearls on an emerald dress.

Across Europe, families gather for their evening meals. Goulash and crepes and pasta and hummus grace the table, while conversations in Hungarian and French and Italian and Greek can be heard debating and arguing and laughing.

In Lesotho in Southern Africa, a woman is taking care of the pumpkin harvest. Although a poor harvest, she shares the largest of the eight pumpkins she has for winter storage with her guest.

Women at the Rhamu market in northern Kenya sit on the ground with their items in front of them, selling milk, sugar, tea leaves, rice, flour, tomato paste, onions, eggs, limes, mangoes, and tiny tomatoes. They chat with each other and with those who come to buy.

At a kibbutz in Israel, the members rise to begin a day of work and sharing, while in Iraq, young children in a Baghdad hospital wake to another day of treatment from caring nurses. On the streets of Calcutta, the dying are met and held by sisters who will be with them during their final moments.

The villages across China come to life, with rickshaw drivers beginning their day and rice field workers heading out to the paddies. In the vertical city of Seoul, businessmen work on economic problems while market vendors descend under the city to sell their wares in the vast underground labyrinth of stores.

Across Lake Atitlan in Guatemala, a lone boat can be seen making its way, the sole occupant listening to the sounds of the forest. Further south, scientists awake to the howling wind and biting cold of the Antarctic, ready to continue their experiments.

In every city and village and town across the world each and every person is welcoming the day or saying goodbye to it in their own special ordinary-but-extraordinary way, using their unique gifts and creating alongside God to make the day a new one once again.

And God smiled and said it was good, and there was evening and morning on the four thousand, seven hundred and eighty-eight trillionth day of creation.

Epilogue

In these pages we've talked about creation being life. Sharing in creation with God is what we are called to do, to use our abilities and gifts to learn more about God and to better our world.

Unfortunately, sometimes people choose not to walk alongside God while they create. Instead they seek to own their creations. They seek power and, as Adam and Eve in that garden of long ago, they seek to be God.

When this occurs, we see the growth of evil. It manifests itself in concentration camps, in calculated murder, in the insanity of war. We see people striving to be God instead of working alongside God with the intention of using creation to know more of this Creator, of this God of Love.

In the face of this misuse of our call to share creation with God, we must use our gift of life, our very gift of creativity, to learn to love as God loves, to do everything for love as God does, and to love enough to triumph over evil and to value all life, all creation as sacred.

Practical Activities

Sometimes we have pushed creativity to the background in our lives and have believed what we have been told throughout the years regarding our lack of creativity. The following exercises may help you reawaken or strengthen that gift from God and will open the door to more ideas of your own!

Moving That Kaleidoscope

Grab a video recorder or a camera; even a sketch book will do and will probably be a better choice if using high tech stuff intimidates you. If sketching isn't for you either, take a tape recorder and a notebook. Pick out some place you haven't been before or pick out some place you have been to quite often (we overlook a lot when we go to a place again and again). Take a walk through this area, stopping to sketch or to take pictures, to talk with the people you meet. Take notes of the thoughts you have or of the nonverbal responses from people. Ask people questions of all sorts, but most importantly, ask them why they are doing something or why they feel a particular way.

When you have completed your walk, go over all your material. Look at it through new eyes and note fresh insights. Go over it again in a day or two. Note how your insights have changed.

Getting in Touch with the Ah Ha Moment

Choose a passage from somewhere in Scripture. Read the passage several times. Now reflect on the moment in several different ways. Consider each person in the moment. What are the challenges each person faces? What are the feelings of each of them? What about the objects in the passage? If you gave them life, what would they say? How would they look in the passage? How would they feel?

Play with it and have fun. After a time consider what particular person or things spoke to you. What struck a chord in you and made you stop and think? What insights did you gain during the process?

Cultivating a Beginner's Mind

This is best done by forgetting who you are. In the following exercise, you are going to put on many different pairs of shoes. What you are going to do is slip into someone else's point of view. First of all, list as many different people as you can think of. Now add the issue or challenge you are in need of addressing. First, what are your thoughts about the situation? Now view the situation through the eyes of each person you have listed. Look at the needs, desires and thoughts of the teenagers, the older people, the teachers— whoever is on your list. Really enter into their thoughts.

Next consider: What will these persons say? What will they do? When you are finished looking through all the points of view, consider the insights you have come up with. What can you learn from these people to help you look at the particular situation in a new way?

Don't forget that the people you choose do not have to be living now. The past can offer us help when it comes to looking at something in a new light.

Law Breaking

For this exercise, list as many laws or rules you can. These might include myths or perceptions or absolutes. You might even consider listing old adages such as "A rolling stone gathers no moss."

Once you have your list, go back and write two ways in which each law or rule can be broken. Too often we accept laws without thinking of why. Consider how breaking some of these laws enables us to consider alternative ways of approaching situations.

Initial Steps

When you want to exercise your creativity in a particular area or deal with a particular situation, one way is to take some initial steps. Simply look at as much stimuli as possible, recording what comes to mind, then see what offers new insight.

First off, gather as much material as possible—books, music, things to touch and smell and taste. Keep in mind the area in which you want to be more creative. Now, without spending too much time on any object or in any area, take in as much stimuli as you can. You are looking only for first thoughts. Perhaps you taste something and a thought occurs. Write it down and move on. Keep focused. Go from stimulus to stimulus, writing each insight as it pops into your mind.

When you are done, you can go through the insights you have garnered. Some will be worth developing, others might have to wait until later, and still others might be discarded. This exercise is not sophisticated, and to some people it sounds childish. Try it, though, and you will find that often the simplest way is the most effective.

Gathering Information

Too often we forget one of our biggest aids to creativity—other people. When you are working on a project and you want to give it a new twist, go and talk with other people. Ask questions to gain any information regarding your topic. Talk to people who will probably not have any preconceived notions of how to approach your topic. Religious educators should try talking to bus drivers or grocery clerks. Ask for their first idea. Talk with them further if you like what you hear. Be open to anything.

The important thing in this exercise is to listen, really listen. Be as open as a child gathering information for the first time. Take it all in. Later consider what was said and use what excites you.

These are just a few exercises that can help jump start you on your way to re-awakening your creativity. Do them and do them often. Also consult the list of resources and begin reading. Above all, trust yourself and your creativity, and trust that God will help you along the way.

Applying Creativity to Faith Formation

These exercises can be used to inject creativity into faith formation. Although they are able to nurture original thinking and activity, creativity lies with us. We are capable of creating our own ways of sharing faith in innovative ways.

- Hold a parade for a special feast or person. Use all sorts of material to make the costumes or the floats.
- Start a never-ending parable that continues from session to session.
- Make "When I Get to Heaven" posters, and discuss everyone's view of heaven.
- Keep a box of various materials to be used for producing various projects.
- Determine some way to value what the learners make—a way to display them or preserve them until the end of the year, when the learners' work can go home with them.
- Gather blankets, pillows, and other materials, and build churches. Talk about how these churches help or hinder community.

- Do experiments connected with faith. Have different liquids represent various people. Have different substances represent occurrences in life. What insights can be drawn from the interaction of life occurrences with individuals? Do all the "people" react the same way to diverse occurrences?

- Use water glasses and make music from them in connection with baptism. The varied levels of water can again represent individuals. You take it from there!

- You or one of your learners may start a drawing while someone else finishes it. This leads into the topic of cooperation and community and what might happen when we don't pay attention to what another has offered. Great discussions can arise from this.

- Pick out a passage from one of the gospels and write it out in a rebus or using pictograms.

- Have a "Fools for Christ" day and have everyone dress as someone who was a fool for Christ or as the fool that they are.

- Collect a random group of photos. Invite the learners to write stories for the photos. Remind them that they are writing about someone who is a member of God's family.

- Fill a grocery sack with at least five different items. Have groups work together to use these items to tell a story of faith, to build something that would help the growth of faith, or to show how God feels about his people.

- Fill a poster board with pictures. Have each child or adult pick out one picture and make as many connections to God with it as possible. Have them do it for community or faith or some other topic.
- Blocks in the meeting space can be used for the tower of Babel, for the Ark, for building a church, and more. Take pictures of whatever creations result.
- Have everyone draw only half of a picture. Assign partners and let each partner imagine what the rest of the picture might be. Exchange sheets after discussing the possible completion of the story, and ask the partners to finish the picture but in another medium. For example, if the first part of the picture was done in crayon, have the partner finish with watercolor or pencil. This exercise lends itself to community and illustrates how difficult it is at times to blend our ideas and thoughts.
- Make a number of finger puppets of biblical figures, holy people, learners of all ages, politicians, workers, and so on. Keep them in your meeting space for creative stories and insights.
- Have the learners write a story about faith in which each line begins with a different letter of the alphabet. Interesting stories emerge, and minds are more active as they wrestle with this challenge.
- Apply faith lessons to different periods of time in history. How did people respond to one another during World War II? How did people worship during the Middle Ages? What did the pioneers do to worship out on the prairie?

- When reading from the Bible, pause and let the learners figure out what might come next. Talk about what the story has to say, and then read the Scripture as it is and see what is the same, what is different, and what new insights have been gained.
- Regularly choose objects to make connections to faith or God, or to other faith concepts. Choose songs and make the same connections.
- Together dance in the classroom. Imagine how David danced before God. Dance the way you imagine Mary did on hearing the good news that Elizabeth was with child.
- Pick a faith word for the day and write it down for you and your learners. Talk about it, dance about it, draw about it. Ingrain that word in your minds.
- Go on a virtual tour of the Holy Land or some other place of faith. Research it and then plan your trip. Imagine whom you meet and what you do. Keep a travel journal.
- Re-create games. How can Charades be played with lives of the saints? How can Hide and Seek be changed into the Shepherd and the Sheep?
- Take everyone outside and let them write in the dirt, imagining what Jesus wrote while the people waited, in the story of the woman caught in adultery.
- Take stop walks. Have the learners stop and enjoy things along the way. They can write down what they see. Invite them to write a brief but thorough description of what thoughts, if any, the objects awaken in them.

- Have a "Why" session. Explore everyone's "why" about certain truths of faith. Talk together about the possible answers. Research if necessary, and keep returning to the "whys."
- Encourage learners to use their imaginations with Scripture. Once you read a passage, have them imagine how the story might have continued. Ask learners to consider what the people in the story may have been thinking.
- Have learners consider different perspectives of the world. Use an object, then ask them what that object would be for someone from South Africa or for a giant or for an eagle. New and interesting observations will occur.

These are just a few of the thousands of twists and turns creativity can bring to faith. Remember that these activities are not limited to children. Adults benefit greatly, as do intergenerational groups who are able to see the wide expanse of ideas these activities offer.

Don't limit God. God doesn't limit us.

Resources

Belliston, Larry and Marge. *How to Raise a More Creative Child.* Argus Communications, 1982

Ealy, C. Diane. *The Woman's Book of Creativity.* Beyond Words, 1995

Ellsberg, Robert. *Blessed Among All Women.* Crossroad Publishing, 2005

Fritz, Robert. *The Path of Least Resistance.* Fawcett Columbine, 1989

Gardner, Howard. *Creating Minds.* Basic Books, 1993

Hainstock, Elizabeth. *The Essential Montessori.* Plume Books, 1986

Hall, Doug. *Jump Start Your Brain.* Warner Books, 1995

L'Engle, Madeleine. *A Circle of Quiet.* Harper Perennial, 1972

Marantz, Robbie. *What Is God?* Firefly Books, 1998

Oech, Roger von. *A Kick in the Seat of the Pants...* Harper Perennial, 1986

————. *A Whack on the Side of the Head,* Warner Books, 1990

Osho. *Creativity: Unleashing the Forces Within.* St. Martin's Press, 1999

Parlette, Snowdon. *The Brain Workout Book.* M. Evans and Company, 1997

Pungente, John and Monty Williams. *Finding God in the Dark.* Novalis, 2004

Stankard, Bernadette. *How Each Child Learns: Using Multiple Intelligences in Faith Formation.* Twenty-Third Publications, 2003

―――. *Prayer and Multiple Intelligences: Who I Am Is How I Pray.* Twenty-Third Publications, 2005

Wakefield, Dan. *Creating from the Spirit.* Ballentine Books, 1996

Wujec, Tom. *Pumping Ions.* Doubleday, 1988

―――. *Five Star Mind.* Doubleday, 1995

Zaleski, Philip and Paul Kaufman. *Gifts of the Spirit.* Harper San Francisco, 1997

O'Brien, David and Thomas Shannon, editors. *Catholic Social Thought: The Documentary Heritage.* Orbis Books, 1992